AF470593

You are not
SPARROWS

S. J. CARR

You are not SPARROWS

A light-hearted account of flying between the wars

LONDON

IAN ALLAN LTD

First published 1975

ISBN 0 7110 0619 9-116/74

Published by Ian Allan Ltd, Shepperton, Surrey,
and printed in the United Kingdom by Morrison & Gibb Ltd,
London and Edinburgh

FOREWORD

Air Chief Marshal
Sir Theodore McEvoy, KCB, CBE, RAF (Rtd.)

'Beau' Carr has sub-titled his book 'A Light-hearted account of Flying between the Wars' and this is apt: our life as junior officers in those days *was* light-hearted. While our seniors were laying the foundations on which our victory in 1945 was built, we rather tended to leave that side of things to them. We lived for flying and, taking no thought for the morrow, asked little more of life in our mid-twenties than to be spared for as long as possible from Marriage and Death.

Iraq, where Beau and I served in the early thirties, was a somewhat monastic existence. Though we had taken no vows, obedience was implicit in our calling, poverty was forced upon us by the 1929 slump, and chastity unavoidable. But the flying more than made up for these austerities.

On the more serious side, this book provides a valuable reminder of the much-misunderstood advantages of 'air-control' in areas where land forces had hitherto had to undertake difficult, expensive and often unrewarding operations. Anyone who cares to read Ludlow-Hewitt's letters in Chapters 6 and 7 will see how humane and economical 'air control' was. Although he doesn't mention it, Beau won the Distinguished Flying Cross for his part in the operations against Shaikh Mahmud. The DFC was so seldom given outside major wars that the reader may be interested in the citation for this particular award:

For outstanding energy, courage and pertinacity throughout the operations against rebel forces in Iraq, in March and April, 1931.
At Awa Barika on 5th April, he carried out, at very low altitude, attacks on hostile forces situated in a ravine—a difficult and hazardous performance in view of the effects of wind eddies on the control of the aeroplane, and the ability of the enemy to fire at close range not only from below but from above the machine —and, after loading up again with ammunition and bombs,

continued the attack while his Commanding Officer was forced to land.

Later in the day he delivered repeated attacks and, when all other aircraft had withdrawn owing to darkness, he continued to cover the operations of the Iraqi troops by machine-gun fire until forced to land in a neighbouring field.

In the opinion of the Officer Commanding, Iraq Army, and the Police, this officer, by covering the advance of the Iraqi troops over open ground assisted materially to minimise the effectiveness of the rebel fire.

One's leisure in those days was occasionally marred by lapses from decorum, of which this book abounds in examples. If the measure now before Parliament which will make it illegal to tell the truth should reach the Statute Book, I shall be able to sue Beau for disclosing my conviction by court-martial. Until then I wish him the best of luck and thank him for reviving so vividly my fading memories of those comparatively carefree days.

Stoke Poges,
28th August 1974.

INTRODUCTION

This book is about aeroplanes. It is also about people, since the one cannot be separated from the other. Throughout I have used actual names, except where to do so might have caused embarrassment. At least half of the people mentioned are dead, and *de mortuis nil nisi bonum*.

Most of the aircraft are dead too, which is a great pity. Many examples of earlier and later aircraft are preserved in public and private collections, notably the Imperial War Museum, the Royal Air Force Museum, and the Shuttleworth Trust; but nowhere in the world, I believe, is there a Wapiti or a Fairey Flycatcher, a IIIF, a Bristol Bulldog or a Hawker Fury, to name but five.

The fighting in Kurdistan was only a very little war, but I have dealt with it at some length, partly because nobody else has thought it worth mentioning, partly because I believed it deserved to be recorded before everybody connected with it was dead and gone, but mainly because it was so very typical of the peace-keeping role of the Royal Air Force throughout the formative years of the 20s and 30s.

Whether we knew it or not, in those two decades between the wars we were training for the big showdown.

With very few exceptions the illustrations are from my own collection of photographs, but I am indebted to, and wish to thank *Flight International* for permission to reproduce the picture of the Hawker Fury, Mr. Brech of the Royal Air Force Museum for locating and lending me the only copy known to exist of the North West Frontier 'goli' (ransom) chit, the Royal Australian Air Force for the photograph of the two Ansons that were landed by one pilot, Patricia Burges, who was the wife of Flight Lieutenant Robinson at the time of his crash at Point Cook, for the loan of the photograph of her late husband's very bent Wapiti, and Adrian Swire for the splendid photograph of his Spitfire going up like a rocket.

Air Chief Marshal Sir Theodore McEvoy was a Flight

Lieutenant at the aircraft depot, Hinaidi, Iraq, when I was in 55 Squadron, and knows as much about Ninaks and Wapitis as anybody. He was also a very fine pilot and continued to fly Spitfires with a physical disability that would have discouraged most people from driving even an invalid carriage.

He transferred from the Depot to 55 Squadron, commanding all three flights in turn, and managed to get himself court-martialled for his (non-active) part in the shooting of Alfie, as related in Chapter 4; a circumstance which did not prevent him from reaching air rank and obtaining a Knighthood.

It used to be said in those far-off days that it was better to be court-martialled than never to be noticed. The theory being that when names cropped up in connection with promotion someone would recall that yes, he had heard of that chap. Must be a good type. Let's promote him. If it was true, they were right about Mac, to whom my thanks are due for writing the foreword, checking the manuscript and correcting the spelling.

Lastly, I should like to thank various girl-friends for typing, re-typing and typing yet again, with infinite patience and fortitude, from my almost illegible hand-written scrawl. But for their encouragement the book, like some aeroplanes I have known, would never have got off the ground.

Knebworth,
Hertfordshire.
1974.

CHAPTER 1

*Leave thine own home, o youth, seek distant
shores! . . .
For thee in Egypt the untroubled lands
Wait, and strange men behold the setting sun
Fall down and rise. Greatly be thou as one
who disembarks, fearless, on alien sands.*

Petronius Arbiter, 1st century AD

Air Ministry, Adastral House, Kingsway, London WC2, February
1929

The very senior officer at the long table managed a frosty smile.
The other six seemed less than pleased to see me.

"What's y'name boy?"

"Carr, sir."

"You address an officer as 'Sir'."

"Yes, sir, I did, sir."

"What did y'say y'name was?"

"Carr"—long pause—"sir."

"Ah, thought y'said Carter, bit deaf y'know, better speak up, lad."

"Yes sir," I bellowed.

"No need to shout, m'boy."

Surely he knew my name. My application form and life history,
such as it was, was right there in front of him.

"Who were the generals at Waterloo?"

"Wellington and Napoleon, sir."

"Any others?"

"Blücher, sir," arrived a bit late.

"Do you play rugger?"—from another member of the board.

"Yes, sir."

"What position?"

"Front row, sir, hooker."

"Play cricket?"

"No, sir."

"Good God, why not, boy?"

The questions came thick and fast from up and down the table.

"How far is the earth from the sun?"
"Ninety million miles, sir, I think."
"What's the distance round the earth at the equator?"
"Twenty-four thousand miles, sir."
"How do you know?"
"Well, I don't really know, sir, but I have always understood it was."
"Don't try to be clever, lad."
"I'm sorry, sir, I thought it was a catch question."
"Never mind, just relax."
"Yes, sir."
"Can you ride a horse?"
"Yes, sir."
"Sail a boat?"
"Yes, sir."
"Drive a car?"
"Yes, sir."
"Shoot?"
"Yes, sir."
"Why do you want to join the Royal Air Force?"
"I want to fly, sir."

A simple enough statement, yet behind it weeks, months, years of day-dreaming.

I had read all the literature, especially the lurid American romanticised accounts of the air war by Elliot White Springs. *War Birds* in particular. I had seen all the films. *Dawn Patrol* three times, in which Basil Rathbone, I think, was the hard-pressed laconic squadron commander and in which Hollywood actors made improbable statements like 'sending kids to their deaths in canvas coffins' subtitled on the silent screen. There was nothing I didn't know about Nieuport Scouts and Spads, Camels and SE5As, Albatrosses and Fokker Triplanes.

My heroes were Mannock, Ball and McCudden. I could have told you all you wanted to know, if you had bothered to ask, about Manfred Von Richtofen, Von Boelcke and Immelmann. Immelmann? I had never been off the ground but I could demonstrate an Immelmann turn with my right hand to perfection.

I had seen Sidney St. Barbe skywriting, advertising Bovril or Player's Navy Cut and earning a precarious living with his old SE5A, and I had been to the RAF display at Hendon.

And then one day it happened. An aeroplane turned up and occupied a corner of a nearby ten-acre cow pasture. The pilot lived in, and used as his office an old army bell tent. He had a camp bed and a couple of boards resting on tea chests for a desk. The notice read 'Joy Rides Five Shillings'. The moment of truth had arrived. The pilot—I never knew his name, perhaps he preferred it that way, and did it matter?—wore oil-stained khaki breeches, lace-up field boots in need of a polish, a once white silk scarf about a mile long, an old RFC maternity jacket (oh joy), less faded where the wings used to be, and over all this a scuffed and torn leather flying coat reaching almost to the ground. On his head a tweed cap turned front to back and a pair of goggles. I could have hugged him.

The aeroplane was a 504K with a Gnome monosoupape rotary engine. Monosoupape? "French for single valve, you fool, get in the front seat," he said, "and don't step on the bloody wing." As if I would. "And don't bloody well touch anything," he added. The seat was of wickerwork, with a black leather cushion cracked and perished with age. He helped me with the seat belt. "Please will you do a loop?" I asked. "No," he said, "not for five bloody bob I won't." It seemed to be his favourite expletive. He climbed into the rear cockpit while his ex-RFC mechanic fussed over him with the seat belt, then moved to the front, and I listened for the first time at first hand to the magic words called and repeated. Switches off. Switches off. Fuel on. Fuel on. Sucking in. Sucking in. The mechanic swung the propellor maybe half a dozen times then, contact. Contact, and with a roar the engine came to life in a cloud of blue smoke and there was that lovely but indefinable stink of burnt castor oil. I sniffed it with distended nostrils like a bird dog pointing a covey of quail. The pilot wasted no time running up. The engine was still warm from the previous flight and in any case, why waste petrol at one shilling and threepence a gallon? We taxied out, turned into wind—there was a wind sock tied to a pole but he called it something rude—and in no time at all it seemed to me the bumping and juddering of the take off run ceased and we were in the air and the ground was falling away. Looking down, everything seemed suddenly toy-like, with doll-sized people, white faces straining skywards looking at me flying at last.

But it didn't really start there. It began years before, in 1917, when I was a small boy. A Camel did a forced landing in a field near the village. Of course I didn't know it was a Camel, not then.

But we saw this aeroplane doing lovely exciting things over the village. Stunting they called it. The pilot had a girl friend who lived nearby, so we learned, in that mysterious way that children have of finding out grown up secrets.

Then the engine stopped and the Camel came lower and lower until it was lost to sight behind a belt of tall elms. "He's going to crash!" we shouted. Dare I say it?—he's going to crash, we *hoped*, and everyone ran to see this tremendous event. Nothing so dramatic as a crash, but exciting enough. There stood the Camel in one of old George Jarvis's fields and the pilot trying to shoo off a couple of dozen cattle.

"I say, you kids, help me keep these bloody cows off my bloody bus, will you?" Cows! we thought disdainfully. Doesn't he know the difference between cows and bullocks? But of course one expected that sort of ignorance on the part of strangers. We had often noticed that visitors, especially those we referred to scornfully as townspeople, seemed not to know the difference between a bullock, a cow or a bull, but we forgave this one. This god-like creature, who must have been all of eighteen years old, who had descended from a blue summer sky in a khaki-coloured flying machine which he called a bus. He could call the cattle Border Leicester sheep for all we cared, and actually to be asked to do something for him, like keeping a few silly bullocks from licking his aeroplane, established a bond of friendship and understanding. "Yes," we said, "there is a telephone in the village. Mr. Jarvis is the nearest one." "Well, one of you come with me to show me the way. The rest stay here and keep the cows away." "Can I come, please?" "Can I come?" "Can I come?"

He was back in about twenty minutes, though it seemed like twenty hours. Questions, questions, questions. Everybody talking at once.

"It's a Sopwith Camel."

"No, I don't know why it's called a Camel."

"I *know* it doesn't look like a Camel."

"Yes, those are guns."

"Vickers guns."

"No, I haven't killed lots and lots of Germans."

"Yes, I am going to kill lots of Germans when I go to France."

"No, I haven't shot a Zeppelin down in flames."

Oh dear, our hero was becoming less godlike every minute.

Well, only a little less. We comforted him and ourselves.

"I bet you shoot down fifty Germans when you go to France."

"I bet he shoots down a hundred."

"Hundreds and hundreds."

"In flames."

We were a bloodthirsty lot.

Now there was another aeroplane coming. It circled the field several times. We could see the pilot quite clearly, looking down. Our friend fished a great fat overgrown sort of pistol thing out of the cockpit. Then he fished around some more and brought out some things which looked like shotgun cartridges, only much bigger, and he put one into the big pistol.

"What is it?"

"It's a Very pistol."

"Can you kill Germans with it?"

"Yes, you could kill Germans with it, but you don't."

"Why is it called a Very pistol?"

"Because it's very big, stupid," said some wag.

He fired into the air and this lovely green rocket thing went hissing and fizzing up into the sky in a great curve and fell back on to the grass, still burning as bright as day. The bullocks went frisking off, tails high and back legs kicking, then stood in a half circle facing us, snorting in shocked surprise. They had never seen a Very light either. The second aircraft came in to land, turned sort of sideways coming over the hedge, straightened out again and was down, then turned towards us, wings swaying from side to side and tail jumping up and down as it bumped across the tussocky turf, turned to face the wind and stopped and out stepped another, much older, god. At least twenty-one, with a moustache. Our friend saluted and called him 'sir'. We were awe-struck and for once silent. Some new drama would now unfold. How, later in this never to be forgotten day, soldiers came in a lorry with a brown canvas top and took the first aeroplane to pieces and packed it all in the lorry and took it away, and how the second god flew away and made a great strong wind and flattened the grass and blew all our hats off, I have no wish to tell, but in 1929 two of my friends joined the auxiliary air force and were learning to fly every weekend and it was absolutely terrific old boy, and why don't you come next week and meet the adjutant—he's a regular, you know—and join too? But no, if I was going to do it I would go the whole hog and be a professional, not a weekend amateur, so here I was in this room being asked all these questions.

"So you want to fly."

"Yes, sir."

"Don't you want to serve your King and country?"

"I suppose so, sir, I hadn't really thought about it."

"You just thought it would be nice to dart about the sky in an aeroplane?"

"Yes, sir."

"Humph . . . Well, wait outside."

Oh hell, no cricket, no King and country. Sunk without trace.

A buzzer buzzed, the orderly ushered me back to a now smiling and affable board and I was handed a chit to take to the Central Medical Establishment. In 1929 nobody had ever heard of personnel selection.

At the CME you stood about for hours stark naked like a skinned rabbit. They checked height, weight, chest measurement and expansion. Tested eyes, ears, nose, throat, lungs, heart, blood pressure, sense of balance, standing on one leg with eyes closed and lots of much ruder things.

From the poker-faced MOs it was impossible to tell whether you were fit to fly or whether you had only six months to live.

So you went home and waited and at last, when you had almost forgotten you had ever applied, and perhaps wished you hadn't, came the buff OHMS envelope, addressed unbelievably to Acting Pilot Officer—they can't really mean it, they must be joking—Carr.

The writer said he was commanded by the Air Council to request that I report to the Royal Air Force depot Uxbridge on April 2nd —not April 1st, so that was something—for two weeks ground training before proceeding—you never *went* anywhere in the RAF, you always proceeded—to Abu Sueir, Egypt, for flying training.

A first class rail warrant was enclosed for the journey to Uxbridge, but no ticket for my Alsatian bitch. But I took her anyway, which was a mistake. Chained up outside the mess one morning, she took a chunk out of the seat of the drill adjutant's beautifully cut breeches as he went by to take the parade.

"Who owns the Alsatian?"

"Me, sir."

"Well, get the bloody bitch off the bloody station immediately and don't come back until you've found another home for her!"

It was a sad parting, but she couldn't have gone to Egypt anyhow.

The entry, as we were called, numbered twenty-two and were as colourful a bunch as you could hope to meet. There was Turner, an old man of twenty-seven, who as a sub-lieutenant in the Navy had fought at Archangel. By natural selection he was appointed senior cadet. There was Wardell, who had been both lumberjack and mountie; Herne, ex-Transjordan Frontier Force; Durben, straight from his parents' Sussex farm; Cauthery, grown tired of his father's Yorkshire woollen mills; and there was Pereira from South Africa.

Uxbridge was drill, during which we learned not to address the warrant officer drill instructor as 'Sir', PT at six in the morning, and lectures on tropical diseases: beri-beri, bilharzia, smallpox, malaria, cholera, elephantiasis, yellow jack and VD. All copiously, too copiously, illustrated by nauseatingly close-up photographs. We were inoculated against three of them and you took your chance with the rest.

All recruit depots in all services are commanded, officered and NCO'ed by sadists, or so it must seem to the recruit. If you doubt it, read *The Mint* by Aircraftman Shaw (Lawrence of Arabia). It is not wholly true of course, yet by definition discipline is strict and punishments when meted out are harsh and where possible designed to fit the crime. Uxbridge was no exception.

The parade ground was vast. It seemed to stretch from horizon to horizon and was sacred ground. It was absolutely forbidden for a recruit to set foot on it unless on parade.

While my course of would-be officers were at Uxbridge a wretched recruit, late for something or other, decided to risk everything and use the parade ground as a short cut. Nor is that all. He sullied the hallowed ground by flinging down a spent match, both of which crimes, of an enormity never previously known to God or man, were spotted by the station warrant officer, who never missed a trick.

Why indeed should he? That's what he was there for.

The airman was placed on a charge and punishment duly awarded, the details of which were left to the devilish cunning of the SWO. It consisted of two-hour periods of drill under a succession of corporal drill instructors, the criminal in full marching order, breeches and puttees, full pack, rifle and bayonet, boots polished to a dazzling sheen, buttons likewise, and webbing equipment blancoed to perfection. This happened three times a day. In between it was working dress and pick up every matchstick on the whole of the vast acreage of Uxbridge camp, scrub each match to a gleaming whiteness and tie them in bundles of twelve. This went on for fourteen days, which was the extent of the award. It might or might not have been a senseless punishment, it might or might not have had sadistic overtones, but of one thing you can be sure, that airman never again walked across a forbidden parade ground and in all probability never again threw down a spent match on air force property.

We 'dined in' and attended guest nights to learn the form and to make sure we knew how to hold a knife and fork and how to behave at table.

There were trips to town to order uniforms from our tailors and to have parties—dinner and cabaret at the Mayfair for 30/–. Or going to Noel Coward's latest play then supper—one dish only but anything that was on the menu, so we always chose caviar, one guinea at the Grosvenor.

There was a uniform allowance of £50 which was supposed to cover the cost of the basic necessities. A paltry sum today, but a lot of money in 1929. It nearly, but not quite, paid for one best blue with slacks and riding breeches, a greatcoat and service dress cap, one pair boots and one pair shoes, two pairs of puttees (one blue, the other khaki), khaki drill tunic and slacks, white shirts and hard collars, khaki shirts, shorts and stockings, leather gloves, a cane and white tropical mess kit.

The only issue items were camp kit, consisting of camp bed, two blankets, canvas wash bowl with folding stand, canvas bucket and a camp stool, all neatly stowed into a valise with stout leather straps and a handle. You learned never to go anywhere without it.

The other was a .455 calibre Colt automatic. I never liked the big heavy Colt which, though a powerful man-stopper if the need arose, was apt to jam if the slightest grain of sand or grit got into the action. So I bought for £3 a .455 Mark VI Webley revolver which packed just as big a punch as the Colt but was better balanced and had a butt which fitted more snugly into the palm of the hand. If anything, it had better stopping power than the automatic because of its lower muzzle velocity and because it used

the plain lead slug, whereas the Colt would only function with a
high velocity nickel-jacketed bullet, which could go right through
the target and out the other side and would not necessarily stop a
determined opponent (though all this of course one was to learn
much later).

We sailed for Egypt in a 7000-ton 7-knot freighter out of
Birkenhead, calling at Gibraltar, Toulon and Naples.

Then Port Said, the harbour full of destroyers of the Mediterranean Fleet. Port Said, of the Gully Gully men doing their
conjuring tricks with eggs, day-old chicks and rabbits; Port Said,
of the filthy picture touts and the pimps entreating all and sundry
to sample the delights of their sisters.

We were taken in tow by a flight lieutenant in shorts, shirt and
topee. Tall, bronzed, moustached and nonchalant, he carried a
horse-hair fly switch with an ivory handle attached to his wrist by
a leather thong. I couldn't wait to get one of those and start
looking like a Sahib.

By train to Abu Sueir, ten miles from Ismailia on Lake Timsah,
half way down the Suez Canal.

Aeroplanes at last; this was what it was all about. This was why
we were here, but not quite yet. Tomorrow perhaps or the next
day.

There was the rest of the course to meet. Seventeen Leading
Aircraftmen from overseas stations, Egypt, the Sudan, Palestine,
Iraq, India, Hong Kong and Singapore, and four Egyptian army
officers, Razik, Haggag, Thami and Mikati. Years later two of
them helped to dethrone Farouk.

We drew our flying kit from stores: helmet and goggles, ear-
phones and Gosport tubes, a khaki denim boiler suit for summer
and a sidcot suit for winter. About now we became aware of the
senior course, flying DH9As and Vickers Vimys and within four
months of completing training and getting their wings. From
them we quickly discovered that an acting pilot officer on probation
of the junior course was the lowest form of pond life.

The course was split between B and E flights, equipped with
Avro 504Ns, the standard RAF *ab initio* trainer. The 504N was
the modified version of the 504K which came into service during
the 1914–18 war; then it had the Gnome Mono rotary engine.
The N which we flew had the Armstrong Siddeley Lynx 7-cylinder
radial rated at 215hp, and was always referred to as the Lynx Avro.

Wing span 36ft; length overall 28ft 11ins; wing loading 7lb per square foot; maximum speed 100mph; cruising 85mph; stalling speed 45mph.

I went to E flight, commanded by Flight Lieutenant Tubby Dawson, later Air Marshal, after whom Dawson Field in Jordan was named, where the Palestinian hijackers blew up the BEA and El Al airliners in 1970.

Each instructor had four pupils; my instructor's name, appropriately enough, was Kirlew. Each flight had its own landing ground in the desert about ten miles from the main aerodrome.

Reveille was at 4.00am, when the native servant appeared with a cup of hot, black, sweet tea. You dragged the boiler suit over your pyjamas, a practice which was frowned on but everybody did it, and marched to the hangars where engines were already started and being run up. The instructors took their first pupils into the air at once while the rest rode out to the LG in 1914 vintage Crossley trucks. From the moment of arrival at the LG tea was brewed by the time-honoured RAF method of boiling a dixie with a blowlamp. The tea was strong, sweet and well stewed, and consisted of about half a gallon of condensed milk and a pound of tea to four gallons of water, something like a tea version of Pussers Kye in the Navy.

This dawn flying routine was general throughout tropical and sub-tropical commands. The day was still cool, there was little if any wind, the sky was cloudless and there was complete absence of turbulence; all of which sounds like mollycoddling, but flying, if not still in its infancy, was then no more than adolescent.

Flight and engine instruments were rudimentary: air speed indicator, altimeter, compass, rev counter, oil pressure gauge and temperature gauge. There were no electrics, no radio, no means of communication with the ground or other aircraft other than hand signals or Very light; every aircraft carried a Very pistol and a stock of red, green and white cartridges.

Intercommunication between pilot and passenger or instructor and pupil was by Gosport speaking tube; it served its purpose well. The Lynx Avro was a forgiving sort of aeroplane, easy to fly but not too easy, and tricky to land cross wind because of its considerable keel surface aft of the centre of gravity.

Flying finished for the day at 7.30am, then bath, shave and dress, while the servant cranked the portable gramophone and changed records. Then breakfast at 8.30, colour hoisting parade and prayers, C of E naturally—fall out the Roman Catholics and Jews, roam out the fallen Catholics, and half a dozen or so would leave the ranks and take station ten paces to the rear, where presumably they were suddenly stricken stone deaf.

9.00am to midday was taken up by lectures: King's regulations, Air Force Law, history of the Royal Air Force—the service was not quite eleven years old but it had a history—customs and etiquette of the service, theory of flight, airmanship, engines and airframes, navigation, meteorology, armaments, and drill and PT. Lots and lots of PT and drill.

We discovered that flying—service flying—was not just for the hell of it. The military aeroplane was a fighting vehicle—a gun platform or a bomb carrier or both—so we learned about ring and bead sights and Constantinesco gear, a device invented by an officer of that name to enable a machine gun to fire through the arc of the propellor without hitting the blades. It was very reliable, but if it did go wrong you could shoot the propellor off. We learned about Vickers guns and Lewis guns and Numbers 1, 2, 3 and 4 stoppages and how to clear them. A pilot in my squadron always carried half a brick in the cockpit. He reckoned smiting the cocking lever of his front gun with the brick was the quickest way to clear any stoppage.

We learned too about ammunition and bombs: armour piercing and incendiary, semi-armour piercing and tracer, detonators and exploders, fuses and high explosive, TNT and amatol, fulminate of mercury and the Wimperis bomb sight.

Gradually too we learned a little about the structure and organisation of the service and how the commands and squadrons were dispersed around the world. Egypt, the Sudan, Palestine, Transjordan, Iraq, Aden, India, Hong Kong and Singapore. We had an empire. Presiding over all this was Sir Hugh, not yet a peer, the great Boom Trenchard, just about to retire but still up there on Mount Olympus.

We began to feel part of it and were proud to be, so we quickly acquired the service slang then current. Thus one hoped not to 'boob' or 'shoot a line' or 'put up a bad show', especially not in front of the 'wogs', but longed for the day when one would be a 'split arse pilot'. A split arse pilot is a skilful fellow good at aerobatics but inclined to be reckless and to show off to any admiring audience, e.g. girl friends. Sooner or later he would kill himself doing just that.

One learned a smattering of Arabic and from the airmen something of that extraordinary mixture of mispronounced Hindi, Urdu, Arabic and Pidgin English with which British troops are able to make themselves understood anywhere east of Gibraltar. So we yelled to Ahmed or Abdul for 'gharam pani jeldi jeldi' when we wished to shave, ordered 'chota pegs' with our 'curry tiffin', and pretended to be frightfully 'mahlish' (which is Arabic for 'manana'), but almost invariable we were answered in English, which is very lowering to the morale of a budding young sahib or effendi.

Average time to first solo was around eight hours and most people got over this hurdle, but not all. There were always a few who lacked the aptitude for flying and these were usually removed from the service without delay, though once in a while a thoroughly 'good type' might be offered the alternative of a transfer to armoured cars, of which the RAF had several companies in desert territories, notably Iraq.

Up to the first solo there were very few incidents, but from that point on some sort of crash, generally of a minor nature, happened almost every day.

I don't know why we broke so many more aeroplanes than they do today. The machines were more fragile of course, and in particular undercarriages lacked any form of hydraulic shock-absorbing device but relied instead on bungie, a sort of overgrown catapult elastic. There was no way of stopping an aircraft if you were running out of airfield, because they had no brakes; moreover, they did not fly themselves—they had to be flown all the time.

For the novice landing was always an adventure, and if you could walk away from it it was a good landing. A good three-point landing, on two wheels and the tail skid, was a source of immense satisfaction, but anything less was horrible to watch and sometimes disastrous. It simply was not done to use the engine on the approach to land. Using the engine on the approach was called 'rumbling' and was looked on as cheating. Once you had throttled back you were expected to stay throttled back; judgement was all. Consequently, if you undershot and tried to stretch the glide by pulling the nose up, an instinctive desire in the novice, more often than not you stalled the aircraft.

If this happened near the ground you generally got away with nothing worse than a damaged undercarriage, but quite frequently you dug a wing into the ground and stood the thing up on its nose or, even more undignified, turned it right over on to its back. These performances were not only seldom if ever fatal, but the occupant nine times out of ten would get out without a scratch.

If the stall took place much higher you either spun in or dived in, a much more devastating business and often fatal. A landing was supposed to be the finish of a journey, not the end of everything.

Engines were less reliable than in later years and forced landings were frequent, so a lot of time was devoted by instructors to teaching good forced landing procedures and techniques, hence the fetish of not using the engine to help the normal approach.

Every landing had to be a forced landing; so judgement of height, speed and distance were the most vital things to learn. Great store was set by 'hands', because an aeroplane responded to the light and sensitive touch; hence the questions at the selection board "Do you sail a boat or ride a horse?"

You did not as now fly by reference to instruments, you flew by feel, you flew by the seat of your pants. You did not sit in or on an aeroplane and drive it, you were part of it, one and indivisible. Flying was still an art and remained so for many years. It did not become a science until after the end of World War II.

We were encouraged to fly the aircraft to its limits, without however overstressing the structure, and to feel at home in every kind of unusual and indeed unlikely attitude. Hence aerobatics; great fun but with a serious purpose, and a sure way of weeding out the ham-fisted.

The 504 was not aerobatic in the fullest sense because it lacked the power to be so. It could not for example perform an upward roll or even a good slow roll, but it did a falling leaf better than any aeroplane I have ever flown. This was pretty to watch and easy to do, even for a novice. It was merely the beginning of a spin immediately checked and initiated again in the opposite direction.

You throttled back, stalled the aircraft from a high nose up attitude, and with the stick held centrally hard back throughout the manoeuvre you applied full rudder; as soon as the wing dropped and the aircraft did a quarter turn of a spin, you kicked on hard opposite rudder to correct that and induce a quarter turn of a spin the other way, and went on repeating the sequence for as long as you wished.

The trouble with it was that you could become mesmerised, or more likely lost in admiration for your own cleverness, thus fail to appreciate the considerable loss of height and go on doing it till you hit the ground. Another disadvantage, again a result of failing to pay full attention, was that the engine would stop, and if you had insufficient height to restart by diving you were stuck with a forced landing.

Very silly you would feel too, standing there in the desert waiting for someone to spot you from the air and wondering what special brand of sarcasm your instructor would have thought up by the time you found yourself face to face.

Throughout this period it paid to be fit and alert; a heavy night and late to bed was not the best preparation for 4.00am reveille and 4.30am take off.

Flight Sergeant Kirlew expressed this very forcibly on one occasion, when some of his pupils reported for flying one chilly dawn with furred tongues and bleary eyes after a party in Ismailia and a visit to that part of town where they had no right to be. "Gentlemen," he roared, "you are not sparrows, you can't fuck *and* fly."

We were taught the best way to crash if a crash was inevitable. For example, a forced landing in impossible terrain. We were shown how at the very last moment to side slip, that is to skid the aeroplane sideways and try to put a wing in first rather than hit the obstruction head on. In theory the wing would crumple and absorb a lot of the shock of instant deceleration, converting forward motion into rotary motion.

All this *ab initio* instruction took place on the Avro 504 and continued for four months. If successfully completed there was two weeks local leave; most people opted for Cyprus, but a few determined to sample the flesh pots of Alexandria and to find out for themselves if it was true that the barmaid at the Bodega had the biggest bust in the business. The bars in Alexandria and Cairo were good places for impecunious junior officers. With your first glass of ice-cold Pilsener the barman brought a huge tray of appetisers: devilled chicken livers, salted pistachio nuts, crisp fried freshly caught sardines, olives and several other goodies, all for free, and he would bring more whenever asked. The beer cost $2\frac{1}{2}$ piastres—tuppence halfpenny, or one new penny.

CHAPTER 2

*Said one—"Folks of a surly Tapster tell
And daub his Visage with the Smoke of Hell;
They talk of some strict Testing of us—Pish!
He's a good fellow, and 'twill all be well."*

Omar Khayyam, tenth century

Now we were the senior course and were permitted to strut. Our knees were brown and our khaki drill had faded and we were flying 'service' types. We no longer looked newly hatched.

The ham-footed and mutton-fisted among us went on to bombers, the twin-engined Vickers Vimy. Those with a lighter touch went on to single-engined aircraft, DH9As and Bristol fighters.

The 9A was born of the unsuccessful DH9, which was intended to replace the DH4 and was designed around a Siddeley Puma engine of 300hp. In the event the Puma never attained its designed power. The production engines were rated at 230hp and thus gave the DH9 shorter range, a lower ceiling and inferior all-round performance to the DH4 it was intended to replace.

Fortunately, at the same time that all this was going on a United States design team had perfected what was then a revolutionary new engine. This was a Vee 12-cylinder liquid-cooled engine of 400hp named 'Liberty', with the two banks of cylinders cast not *en bloc* but separately, each with its own water jacket.

The decision was made at Trenchard's insistence (who else?) to order this engine in quantity and the contract for producing the airframe to take it was awarded to the Westland company at Yeovil, Somerset.

In fact, Westlands found it necessary to re-design the DH9 almost entirely to take the new engine. They gave the aeroplane wider span, greater chord and increased wing area, and it was re-designated 9A.

There were the usual teething troubles, as a consequence of which the war was almost over before the first operational squadron was equipped. This was 110 Squadron at Kenley. They received their first batch in late June 1918 and by mid-August had their full complement of eighteen, all of which had been paid for and donated by His Serene Highness the Nizam of Hyderabad.

The squadron moved to Bettoncourt in France and their first operational sortie was a raid on Boulay aerodrome on September 14th. Only three other squadrons were equipped with the type by the time of the Armistice, so the 9A did not have any decisive effect on the war.

A few saw service in 1919–20 with the RAF training mission in Russia, assisting the abortive White Russian resistance to the Bolsheviks, but the 'Ninak' as it became known really came into its own throughout the twenties in Iraq, India, Palestine and Transjordan. It was to remain a front-line aircraft until the early thirties.

The 9A was non-aerobatic and had a vicious spin in which it lost a lot of height very quickly. Not that this prevented the over-confident from trying to show off.

There was one grisly incident in which someone tried what turned out to be a very unpolished attempt at a loop. He dived the thing to well above its safe maximum speed to ensure getting round, hauled the stick hard back and the wings came off at the top of the loop. He went on down vertically in the fuselage until the ground got in the way.

Of all the eighty or so types of aircraft I have flown in my time the DH9A required more nicety of judgement and precision of handling for a landing than any, which is one reason why it was a good training aeroplane. If you were a fraction too fast on the approach it floated for ever right across the airfield, and if you were a mite too slow it fell out of your hands just as you started to hold off. If you held off high and dropped it, the resultant bounce could be twenty feet or more. If you misjudged it the other way and flew it into the ground wheels first with the tail well up, the same thing happened, but you had more speed in hand for recovery, though even then you had to be quick.

The approach to land in the 9A called for fully retarded ignition and one switch off, otherwise the tick-over was too fast and so was the speed. So to go round again after a bounce meant switching on that switch, advancing the ignition, opening the throttle wide and re-trimming, in that order, and there was not much time for any of it. If you got it wrong and opened the throttle before switching on and advancing the ignition, the engine would fail to respond and you were in big trouble.

Add to all this that great long snout, with its huge flat-fronted radiator stuck out in front completely obscuring the forward view, and you can imagine what a handful of aeroplane you were wrestling with. Yet to put a 9A on to the ground properly in a perfect three-pointer was very satisfactory. I can recall no other aeroplane in forty-five years of flying that gave such a feeling of accomplishment in not only putting it down properly but precisely where you wanted to.

The DH9A, officially designated a general purpose and day bomber aircraft, came into service in 1918 and remained in squadron use right up to 1931. It was a good aeroplane, and because it was not too easy to fly, a good training aeroplane, but it probably killed more trainee pilots than most, mainly because it so often caught fire in even a minor crash. Its Liberty engine had coil ignition which of course required a battery. The non-spill battery had not yet been invented, so in a crash or bad landing, if the aircraft ended on its nose at or over the vertical or flat on its back, battery acid spilled out on to a hot exhaust, was converted instantly to gas and exploded, thereby making certain of setting off any spilled fuel, even if that had not started to burn in its own right. Being a wood and fabric aircraft, or 'stick and rag' as they call it nowadays, the result can be imagined. Also being a wooden aircraft, if it did go right over on to its back the centre section usually collapsed and you couldn't get out.

A mild prang in a Bristol fighter was not all that funny either. The butt of the forward firing Vickers gun stuck out through the instrument panel just nicely in line with the forehead, nose or chin of the pilot, depending on how tall he was, so there were plenty of pilots walking about with a 'Brisfit' chin or nose.

It was not only the pilots under instruction who broke aeroplanes; the instructors were quite capable of doing it themselves. During my time at Abu Sueir three instructors were killed, two in mid-air collision and one who spun in from 2000 feet.

We became expert at the slow march and resting on arms reversed, and the station band's rendering of the Dead March from *Saul* could hold its own with the best, yet oddly enough none of this had much effect on anyone. Not that we were especially callous, but after all it couldn't happen to you; it would always be the other fellow, poor chap, and the immediate reaction of all and sundry was to rush to the spot and photograph the wreckage.

Although people *did* kill themselves, most of the crashes were minor and many were more comic than tragic.

One such was a classic. A pupil on the junior course, who had had hours of dual and quite demonstrably showed little aptitude for flying, seized what must have seemed a heaven-sent opportunity to 'show 'em'. His instructor, Firpo Chichester, a 6ft 4in 17-stone heavyweight boxing champion and front row forward, after half an hour of fruitless endeavour one morning landed his Avro, got out, leaving the engine ticking over, and with full modesty, blanketed by the rudder, did a piddle. Choosing the absolutely right psychological moment, the pupil slammed the throttle wide open for take off, giving Firpo the full slipstream and a face and crotch full of sand, as he stood there aghast with his mouth wide open and both hands full.

The Avro did a wide ground loop on full left rudder with the stick hard forward, until the starboard wing tip and then the prop hit the ground and the whole thing cartwheeled over and ended up flat on its back, thus concluding yet another promising service career.

A frequent cause for merriment was when in some minor landing mishap the aircraft came to rest on its nose but over the vertical and the pilot, glad to find himself alive and forgetting he (a) was upside down and (b) ten feet from the ground, pulled the quick release pin from his Sutton harness and fell straight out of the cockpit on to his head.

Looking back on it, I cannot think why we were so daft and irresponsible. Not only the pupils and flying instructors. A ground instructor armourer for example, one of the people who live with and handle explosives all the time, got very blasé. He was lecturing the course on detonators, holding one for all to see and explaining that it was filled with fulminate of mercury. Then, tossing it nonchalantly from one hand to the other and back again, he said, "This is the most sensitive explosive there is; it can be set off just by the heat of the hand." And my God it did exactly that, and blew off half his hand.

Occasionally some strange civilian aircraft dropped in from the outside world. One day in late December a lanky bespectacled young New Zealander named Francis Chichester arrived in a funny little De Havilland-built aircraft called a Gipsy Moth. He said he had flown out from England and was hoping to get to Australia.

We thought he was out of his mind but, as all the world knows, he did get there. All his single-handed sailing epics, right up to the time he died, were made in little ships called Gipsy Moth.

Then two Australians, Piper and Kay, turned up in an even queerer aeroplane, a Desoutter high wing monoplane. They too were heading for home and succeeded. It was an era of record-breaking flights. Flight Lieutenant Orlebar had just broken the speed record by achieving 357.7mph in the Schneider Trophy seaplane, the Supermarine S6 with a Rolls Royce 'R' engine. This was Mitchell's design and foreshadowed the Spitfire. A little later an American, Lt. Soucek of the US Navy, set a new altitude record of 43,154.9ft in a Wright Apache with the 450hp Pratt and Whitney engine. But much more exciting to us than the occasional appearance of some misguided civilian was the arrival at Port Said of the aircraft carrier *Courageous* of the Mediterranean Fleet, when its entire complement of aircraft spent two weeks visiting all the RAF stations in Egypt.

Strange looking aeroplanes with exotic roles and unlikely names. Fleet spotter reconnaissance, torpedo bomber, fleet fighter: respectively the Fairey IIIF, the unlovely and misnamed Blackburn Dart and the tiny broken-backed-looking Fairey Flycatcher, of tremendous aerobatic capability and that marvellous 'blue' note of its stub exhaust engine and the prop tips when it pulled out of a dive.

We engaged the Navy at rugger, hockey and boxing, gave a cocktail party and finished up with a guest night which, as always, produced many more broken bones than any field game.

It was sobering to learn that more than half the pilots in the Fleet Air Arm were RAF officers.

Organised games were compulsory in all the services. You had to play something, however bad you might be at it or however much you might dislike it. In fact, everybody had their particular thing which they did like and were good at. Mine happened to be swimming and rugby football. There were ample opportunities for both. Service rugby in the Middle East reached a high standard and was a very fast game, principally because of the nature of the pitch, which was the desert sand picked clean of every stone or pebble, however small—native labour was cheap and plentiful—then copiously soaked with used aero-engine oil and rolled. It sounds awful, and the smell under the North African sun could be nauseating, but it produced a splendid playing surface, firm yet yielding, though abrasive when you were brought down hard.

Sand yachting was popular and this was the ideal country for it. There seems to be an impression current that sand yachting is a recent invention, yet it was in full swing in the RAF in the early twenties. Mainly it was a preserve of the troops, no doubt because only they had the skills to build the yachts, which they did from the unlimited supplies of wrecked aircraft. There were thirty or forty such outfits at Abu Sueir in 1929.

Officers under instruction were not allowed to own motor cars or motor cycles. Not that it mattered; taxis were cheap and you drove them yourself anyway.

Every afternoon there would be a fleet of taxis, mostly open four-seater Fiats, lined up outside the mess waiting to carry the young effendis to Ismailia or wherever. The routine never varied. Two of his passengers would haul the protesting driver out of his seat at the wheel while a third slid into his place, upon which the wretched man would go down on his knees and call Allah to witness that his four wives and twenty children would starve if the sahibs wrecked his car, and we would be off with Abdul on the running board clinging on as best he could. I can't think what the Race Relations Board would make of it.

Ismailia provided a change from mess food in the few hotels that were in bounds, usually the misnamed 'Splendide', and also such modest shopping as we required. The shops were good, many of them colonial branches of famous Paris stores, but not much good to us, on twelve shillings a day pay. But there was always Lake Timsah with its unlimited sailing and swimming. We also swam in the canal, but this could be dangerous when a ship came through. A great wall of water engulfed you as she approached, and was then sucked away, and you with it if you were not careful, as she passed. Another less pleasing sight in the Suez was the occasional bloated dead body floating past covered with prawns. We didn't care much for prawns in Egypt.

Social life was very limited and girls non-existent; night spots there were none. Ismailia was the headquarters of the Suez Canal Company and, apart from Arab town, was wholly French.

We were honorary members of the Cercle Français, at which there was a dance every Saturday night. A very formal affair in which the girls sat demurely with hands in lap and downcast eyes,

You asked Maman if you might dance with Celeste or Monique or whatever the wretched girl's name was, and under the eagle eye of Maman you plodded round the floor to music from one of those excruciating French squeeze-box dance bands with your partner practically at arms length. When the music was mercifully at its temporary end, you returned Michelle to her parents and retired with as much dignity as you could muster, which wasn't much.

The only girls in the whole of Ismailia with whom it was possible to have any social contact were the B...... twins, Molly and Pat, daughters of a retired English sea captain now a Suez canal pilot. The twins were handed on from course to course, for I don't know how many years. I believe at least one, but probably both, eventually married into the RAF.

Social life on the station was conducted strictly in accordance with the manual on *Etiquette of the Service*. There was a married patch known—what else?—as Clover Town. The officers who occupied these quarters—again by the rule book, but King's Regulations and Air Council instructions this time—were of or above the rank of Flight Lieutenant or over the age of thirty. If you were neither of these things, you did not qualify for marriage allowance and could not occupy a married quarter. In official eyes you were living in sin. It was not a bad system. It was designed to ensure as far as possible that a young officer lived the first five or ten years of his service in the Mess, where he would be most likely to learn his job properly, and being on station he would learn to know his men well and they would get to trust him.

Moreover, he was not distracted by the burden of domesticity and was not tempted to get the hell off the station at 4.30pm every day. In short, he was on duty twenty-four hours a day. I could see nothing wrong with it.

Four subjects were taboo in the Mess: religion, women, politics and shop. The first three quite clearly had their origins in the days when tempers were short, the port was good and a duel was the quickest way of settling a quarrel; but why discussion of the profession to which you belonged was discouraged, apart from the risk of boring everybody to tears, I never really discovered, but it was certainly considered bad form to do so.

Back to Clover Town. New arrivals were expected—indeed it was mandatory—to call on all the married officers. Strictly this was supposed to be done within ten days of arrival. The system as it affected us was cut and dried. On a pre-arranged day you got all tarted up in your best Tussore silk tropical suit and brown and white co-respondent shoes, smarmed your hair down in the fashion of the late twenties, and humming 'Tea for Two' set off with a wallet full of cards to OMQ.

The custom was to leave two cards, one for himself and one for his lady. In theory your knock on the door would be answered by the Sudanese servant, who would usher you into the drawing room, dropping your two cards on the silver tray in the hall, and after a suitable interval Madame would appear, all slinky in an afternoon dress, and there would be tea and tête-à-tête. At this rate of progress you might manage one call per afternoon and not complete the task for several weeks.

As I said, it was all pre-arranged. The ladies—all of them—knew you were coming, so the little sliding board by the front door which said 'in' or 'out' read 'out'. You knocked anyhow and the door opened instantly as if by magic. Your advance had been noted and there stood the Sudanese, all handlebar moustache and red tarbush, silver tray in hand. You put the cards on the tray, retreated and repeated the performance fifteen more times. That was it; you had discharged your social obligations in an afternoon.

The next move in this charade would be an invitation to tea, half a dozen at a time like schoolboys. You probably never met again, except possibly at a cocktail party or the Christmas fancy dress dance, or if you happened to play tennis. Never mind, go and cry on Molly's shoulder—or was it Pat's?

The course ended with a series of tests. Full load test, height test (15,000 feet minimum with a sealed height-recording barometer in the back—no oxygen—never heard of it), and cross country navigation test, or air pilotage as it was called. You did a dual with the navigation instructor, one Somerset Thomas, ex-RN. Perhaps the RAF were not so hot on navigation.

This test was easy, as it was quite impossible to get lost. Abu Sueir to Heliopolis via Tel El Kebir; on the outward leg you kept the desert to starboard and the Sown to port; on the return leg what else but the other way about.

Written exams. They took a week, mornings only, all the subjects. Misery! Turner had a large thermos flask of cold gin and lime each day. The invigilating officer thought it was water.

Then the final crunch—flying test with the chief flying instructor.

Not Theodore Quintus Studd (he had gone), but Charles Roderick Carr. He didn't do me any favours.

Then the great day. Passing out parade. Best blue—it was winter now—breeches and puttees, leather gloves, cane held smartly under the left arm, aircraft all spit and polish and lined up; award of wings. One of the gods came down from on high for that—Francis Scarlett, Air Officer Commanding Middle East. One became the trusty and well beloved servant of George, by the grace of God, Rex and had a roll of parchment to prove it.

It was all over. We had made it. Dismiss. Mad rush to the notice board to read the posting list:

Alexander	216 squadron, Heliopolis, Egypt.
Banks	11 squadron, Risalpur, North West Frontier Province, India.
Collins	60 squadron, Kohat, North West Frontier Province, India.
Carr	55 squadron, Hinaidi, Iraq.

A howl of joy went up from the airmen pilots. They were old hands, they'd been around.

"Poor old Carr."

"You'll come back with a squeaky voice—*if* you come back."

"Don't force land."

"It's the women that do it, you know."

"Do what, you idiots?"

"Cut 'em out with a rusty knife."

"Yes, if you're lucky."

"More likely smear 'em with honey and tie you down over an ant hill."

Surely it couldn't be true, could it? They were joking, but I wasn't sure. I was even less sure when I did get to the squadron and found, among the few items issued, a document described irreverently as a 'Goli chit'. It was in Turkish, Arabic and Persian, and promised to my captors the magnificent sum of twenty gold Turkish Mejidies if I was returned unharmed to the nearest British military unit. So that's all I was worth to His Majesty's Government. A miserable twenty quid. It was no comfort to learn that none of the tribesmen could read, but all that came later.

Yet despite the teasing by the airman pilots I was very happy about my posting. I had heard a lot about 55 during my short time in the service; who hadn't? Their exploits in the deserts of Iraq and the mountains of Kurdistan were legendary. Their motto *Nil Nos Tremefacit*, 'nothing daunts us', freely translated by the troops as 'you can't put the wind up 55', was going to take some living up to.

They were reckoned to be a crack squadron. Subsequent events led me to wonder whether that descriptions should not have been amended to read crackpot.

The 'fighting fifty-fifth' had never served at home. They were formed in Turkey in 1917, at about the time I was helping to prevent some cattle from eating a Sopwith Camel, and had been on active service in the Middle East ever since. They remained overseas right up to and after the last war, the end of which found them in Italy.

The last I heard of them they were flying Victor tankers, refuelling Lightnings and at long last stationed in the UK, which sounds a boring sort of pastime.

Ulysses, in another context, had a word for it:

How dull it is to pause,

To make an end,

To rust unburnished,

Not to shine in use.

There was twenty-one days' leave before reporting for duty to the squadron. Time enough to get to England and back, but not by sea, which in any kind of ship I could afford would take ten days each way.

CHAPTER 3

Now that these wings to speed my wish ascend,
The more I feel vast air beneath my feet,
The more toward boundless air on pinions fleet,
Spurning the earth.

Giordano Bruno, sixteenth century

Getting from Egypt to England and back was no great problem, even if you could not do it in style. Deck passage by Messageries Maritimes to Venice, second class on the train the rest of the way; the same thing in reverse. Then you took the train from El Kantara to Haifa, travelled 300 miles in a wog taxi from there to Damascus, but with no notion of how to cross the 500 miles of desert between Damascus and Baghdad.

There was a way, two ways in fact, but I couldn't afford either. One was to take the once-weekly bus, run by two New Zealanders —Nairn Eastern Transport Overland Desert Mail. The other was the irregular air service operated by a French outfit which might or might not have a serviceable aircraft.

After three days of bumming around I fell in with some French Foreign Legionnaires, and they introduced me to some Arab merchants who had hired a Buick with driver for the journey. They agreed to let me join them. Surface travellers were regularly shot up by the Bedouin, but the risk had to be accepted. That was a lousy trip. Jammed in the back seat of an open tourer between two of the fattest Arabs imaginable, under a scorching sun in a permanent cloud of dust, the journey took two days. All we had to eat was water-melon—their water-melons—but we did not get shot up, though we saw some ridden camels on the horizon and sent a signal to Allah.

We did get a meal and kip at night. Rutbah, just inside the Iraqi frontier with Syria, was a fortified caravanserai of great antiquity, with a company of Camel Corps and a posse of native desert police. There was water for a bath, food of a sort and a charpoy.

The usual dawn start, and somewhere around mid-afternoon we

were skirting Lake Habaniya, a vast stretch of brackish water where six years later the RAF built a great air base when Hinaidi was handed over to the Iraqi Air Force. Towards late afternoon the mirage of Baghdad appeared well above the horizon, though it was probably still fifty miles away. Away to the north the Holy City of Khadimain, the four great domes of the mosque covered with gold leaf gleaming like satellite suns.

At last Baghdad, no longer a mirage: the Arabian nights, Haroun al Rashid, Scheherazade, strings of camels forty strong, with that long, slow, rocking gait and the look of disdain. He looks like that because man knows only ninety-nine names for Allah, but the camel knows a hundred. They carried enormous loads— of what?—spices from India, silks from Afghanistan, carpets from Bokhara, Samarkand and Isphahan. Flying carpets, without doubt. I wondered how long it took to go solo on one of those. The camelteers were armed to the teeth, with long curved knife at the waist, bandoliers of ammunition and long-barrelled rifles.

Now the city proper. Men sitting outside the Chaikhana drinking tea and smoking the hooka; in the street were women—one *supposed*, you couldn't really tell. Great fat shapeless creatures dressed in black from head to foot, with just a slit for the eyes, carrying their shopping on their heads.

The romantic image was fading. That all-pervading stink of the East, compounded of camel dung, sun-dried slops, excrement, spices and ancient fish. Beggars everywhere with malformed limbs and obscene sores. Baksheesh sahib, alms for the love of Allah.

We drew up at the Maude Hotel overlooking the Tigris. I was not due to report till tomorrow, which was just as well. Dirty, scruffy, unshaven, tired and hungry. Bath, dinner and bed; Baghdad could wait.

A taxi, Model T Ford, took me the ten miles to Hinaidi. A huge station housing command HQ, an aircraft depot, a hospital, a battalion of Syrian levies, two sections of armoured cars, and until quite recently five squadrons. However, No 1 fighter squadron, flying Sopwith Snipes, had been disbanded to re-form and re-equip in England. 8 squadron had gone to Aden and 45 to Heluan in Egypt. Now there was only 70 Bomber Transport Squadron and my own 55.

Even on a multi-squadron station, each squadron was inde-

34

pendent and autonomous. It had its own officers, NCOs and airmens' messes and quarters. It serviced its own aircraft with its own troops and lived and worked by its own rules. There was no stuffed-shirt Group Captain station commander breathing down our collective necks. We bent the knee to only one god: the squadron commander.

The arabanshi knew the way to 55 squadron. I reported to the adjutant on arrival and got a shock.

"There's no-one about, old boy," said he. "The squadron's on operations in the Southern desert. A bit of trouble with the Akhwan and the Wahabi. You are posted to B flight, commanded by Flight Lieutenant 'Dolly' Gray. We're re-equipping with Wapitis, but I'm afraid you will be on 9As for a few weeks.

"Your aeroplane is in the flight hangar and your air gunner, Corporal Bailey, is standing by. I suggest you get a bit of flying practice and then tomorrow you are to fly down to Busaihia Fort to join the squadron. It's about 300 miles south. You might need this."

He handed me a sheet of paper printed in three languages. Oh my God—the Goli chit. So soon? What good could I do against the Akhwan. Me, who had not yet fired a front gun or dropped a bomb, not even a practice bomb, nor ever flown in formation. And how the hell was I supposed to find a pin-point in thousands of square miles of sweet damn all? Me, who had done one solo cross-country—Abu Sueir to Heliopolis and back in fifty miles visibility. But I hadn't reckoned with Corporal Bailey. Thank heaven for all the Corporal Baileys that ever were.

These men, good craftsmen, intelligent, experienced, good-humoured and loyal, did more to guide, reassure and give confidence to green young pilots than all the regulations, Air Council instructions and training manuals put together. How they could so cheerfully fly with such raw, inexperienced new boys as myself, I cannot imagine.

Corporal Bailey introduced himself to me and me to my aircraft —his aircraft. He was fitter as well as air gunner.

This 9A looked different from the trainers. More aggressive and business-like, it carried much more equipment. There were guns; the front Vickers gun fixed and firing through the airscrew arc. The belt of .303 ammunition carefully graded—one tracer, one semi-armour piercing, one incendiary and so on—neatly folded in the ammo box so that it would run smoothly. The rear Lewis gun, on a Scarff ring mounting, with one pan of ammo in position and eight or nine others clipped on to spigots around the inside of the gunner's cockpit.

There were bomb racks beneath each lower main-plane. Slung one each side of the rear cockpit there were charguls, water bottles made of canvas which allowed their contents to seep constantly through and thus, by evaporation and with the help of the aircraft's slipstream, provided cooling. There were emergency rations in the locker: tins of Maconachies meat and veg., sardines, bullybeef, hard tack biscuits, condensed milk and Horlicks malted milk tablets. There were iron screw pickets lashed to each wing-tip skid, and engine and cockpit canvas covers stowed in their locker. This aeroplane had an extra tropical radiator fitted below the engine nacelle, and it also carried a spare wheel. Camel thorn was the one thing that grew in the desert and punctures were frequent.

This was my aeroplane, my very own, by kind permission of Corporal Bailey.

Navigating to Busaihia presented no problem to Bailey. He had been there several times. After about 200 miles he said, "If we are on course" (I liked that 'if') "you'll see a patch of paler coloured desert to starboard. Keep it starboard for the next half hour and you'll be okay. I'll tell you when to start losing height. Don't worry, I know this lousy bloody country like me own backyard. This time of year it should be okay, if we took off about 09.00 hours, with a bit of luck we'll be there by lunchtime. Would you like to try the kite out now, sir?"

"Yes please, corporal."

So we did a few circuits and landings to get the feel of it, then floated around to learn the landmarks.

The cantonment of Hinaidi, as big as a town, was on a bend in the Tigris, at its confluence with the Diyala river. Baghdad, to the north-west, was dominated by the huge mosaic domes of the Blue Mosque, and due south about twenty miles lay the Arch of Ctesiphon, impressive relic of an earlier civilisation, alongside which were the squadrons' bombing and air-firing ranges. There was a narrow green strip of cultivation along both banks of the two rivers and everywhere else, from horizon to horizon, the bare, brown, stony, basalt desert.

36

Next morning we stowed our camp kit and the extra rations we had drawn for the trip, started up with the help of the Hucks and we were away.

Dutifully, I had drawn a line representing our track on the map, but once the river was left behind it meant nothing to me. There were no landmarks, just desert, and I hoped I could steer a steady compass course and correct for drift. But secretly I was relying utterly on Corporal Bailey, though in course of time one learned to read the desert as a fly fisherman learns to read the water. There are waddies, bits of higher ground and depressions; landmarks enough, which you subconsciously memorise.

The rest was anti-climax. The squadron in general, and my flight commander in particular, didn't want me. I was quite useless to them and anyhow the tribal uprising had been put down. I was supposed to be back at base doing orderly officer. Someone had blundered.

But they were kind to the new boy. There was a party that night to celebrate the end of a little desert war (there was almost always a party for some reason or other, or for no reason whatever) and I heard, for the first of many times, the squadron song. It had a moral:

> In the year anno domini one nine two four
> Up in Sulaimaniya there started a war
> And squadrons of bombers sailed into the sky
> To beat up the A-rabs and give them Kai-ai.
> *Chorus:*
> No balls at all, no balls at all,
> If your engine cuts out,
> You'll have no balls at all.
>
> There was a pilot who went to bomb Sul,
> His bombs were all right but his tanks they weren't full.
> The airgunner's voice thru' the phones clear did call
> "If you engine cuts out you'll have no balls at all."
> *Chorus:* No balls, etc.
>
> They were just over Sul when the engines cut out,
> Again from the rear came that agonised shout,
> "If you land to the south of the Barzan pass

You can stuff your old Lewis gun right up your arse."
Chorus: No balls, etc.

They looked down below and there plain to see
Was Shaikh Mahmud and his party to tea,
Sitting around midst the stones and the rocks
Discussing spring fashions and pruning gents' cocks.
Chorus: No balls, etc.

They landed and ran like the chaff 'fore the wynd,
That bowie knife party six inches behind.
They knew they were in for some terrible shocks
So they banged out their bollocks on sharp stony rocks.
Chorus: No balls, etc.

Sotto St. Peter reclined on a fleecy white cloud,
 voce: The orderly angel came hovering around,
He said to St. Peter, "It's quite plain to me
That here is a signal that you ought to see.
It's from Aero 5, today's date, and to say
That an old DH9A is coming this way."
Chorus: No balls, etc.

They went down to the drome in the midst of the night,
They laid out the flarepath and set it alight,
They pooped off the Very lights, red, green and white,
To show them the wynd ere they should alight.
Chorus: No balls, etc.

Fal- They came in to land, they were full of good cheer,
setto: St. Peter said "Boys, shall we split the odd beer?"
The pilot replied, in a voice clear and shrill
"Thank you, St. Peter, I think that we will."
Chorus: No balls, etc.

The moral of this is quite plain to see;
Look after your petrol wherever you be
And if midst the Kurds and the Arabs you roam,
If you must have 'em out, have 'em cut out at home.
Chorus: No balls, etc.

38

The improbable inclusion in the party of a Bedouin tribesman speaking impeccable English lent an air of incongruity to the proceedings, more especially as he contributed to the singing with gusto. It was the political officer, an RAF flight lieutenant, who lived there in that grisly fort in the middle of the desert, as one with the tribesmen. He had been there for years and he loved it. The only thing he ever asked for was gin and fresh bread. The squadron saw to it that he got it whenever possible. Frank Wooley justified his need for gin by two quotations from what he called his 'private' copy of the Koran: "Man cannot live by bread alone", and "the wages of gin is breath". I imagine he needed his philosophy to cope with the Akhwan, that fanatical warrior tribe who lived by raiding, despised the infidel Ferangi—us—and acknowledged allegiance only to Allah.

It is a reasonable supposition that, without the far-sightedness of Trenchard and the experience the Royal Air Force gained in the twenties and thirties, the Battle of Britain ten years later might never have been fought. There was scarcely a time during these two decades when the RAF did not have a war of some sort on its hands, either in the Middle East or on the North West Frontier of India.

Until the 1914–18 war the whole of the Middle East, including Egypt, Mesopotamia, Syria, Palestine, Transjordan, and Lebanon, had been part of the Ottoman Empire, but with the defeat of the Turks this whole vast area degenerated into a cockpit of disorganised, undernourished, quarrelsome tribes and ambitious Shaikhs.

In an effort to stabilise the situation the League of Nations devised a plan whereby certain of the great powers would be given a mandate to govern these states, with the intention of leading them as quickly as possible to independence.

Great Britain assumed responsibility for the security and political integrity of Mesopotamia (Iraq), Palestine and Transjordan, while France accepted the mandate for Syria and Lebanon.

For this task the British had a garrison, based mainly on Hinaidi, near Baghdad, of one British and one Indian army division, a brigade of native levies, mostly cavalry, and four RAF squadrons.

With this inadequate but expensive force they were expected to police a million square miles of desert and mountain and some thousands of miles of ill-defined frontier.

As always, there was pressure at home to 'bring our boys back' and let the Middle East sort out its own problems. To have done this would have been to condemn the countries to wholesale slaughter, and possibly given the Turks the excuse they needed to re-occupy the territories. They had plenty of friends among the leading Shaikhs to assist them.

As so often in the past, Trenchard had a solution. He proposed a system of air control whereby the RAF should replace the army and thus reduce the military expense to a fraction of what it took to maintain the existing ground forces.

There were many who considered it could not be done, and just as many, I suspect, who hoped it couldn't, but Trenchard's plan was accepted. The army was withdrawn, except for the native levies, the RAF was assigned what was called a peace-keeping role, for which purpose its strength was increased to eight squadrons plus four squadrons of armoured cars, and the first ever system of garrisoning a country from the air was under way.

The squadrons selected for the task were numbers 70 and 45 bomber transport, equipped with Vickers Vernons, numbers 8 and 30 general-purpose day bomber squadrons, with DH9As, and number 1 fighter squadron with Sopwith Snipes, all stationed at Hinaidi. Number 6 squadron of Bristol Fighters was at Kirkuk in Kurdistan, and number 55 at Mosul, near the Turkish-Kurdish border, and 84 squadron at Shaibah, in the south, were both equipped with 9As.

That was in 1922. By 1930, so successful had the system proved that the force had again been reduced and the entire job was now carried out by five squadrons with six sections of RAF armoured cars.

Number 1 fighter squadron had gone back to England, number 6 was at Ramleh in Palestine, number 8 was in Aden, and number 45, which had changed its role from transport to light bomber and equipped with the Fairey IIIF, was at Helwan in Egypt. 30 and 55 squadrons, for some obscure reason, merely swapped stations.

The fifth squadron was number 203 flying boat, equipped with Supermarine Southamptons and based at Basrah on the Shat-el-Arab. Their task was different and, apart from 'showing the flag' flights all around the Persian Gulf, consisted largely of co-operating with the Navy to prevent gun-running and slave trading between Somalia and Arabia.

40

The troops of 203 squadron said of Basrah that the Persian Gulf was the arse-hole of the Empire and Basrah was 500 miles up it, a sentiment shared by everyone who ever visited the place.

During this early period of air control, another and perhaps more significant demonstration of air power took place. At about the time my course were square-bashing at Uxbridge, the first air evacuation of a beleaguered city was coming to an end.

In Afghanistan the Shiamwari tribesmen had rebelled against King Amanullah, invested Dakka and cut the road and all communications between Kabul and the Khyber Pass. Eventually Kabul itself was attacked and the British Legation was cut off from the city.

It was decided to try to evacuate the women and children by air. The only squadron with suitable aircraft was number 70 at Hinaidi, by then equipped with Vickers Victoria troop transports. The squadron flew from Iraq to Risalpur and from there operated a shuttle service over mountain country in one of the worst winters on record, rescuing 586 people of many nationalities. Perhaps the great Berlin Airlift owed something to that.

By 1930 the major frontier wars had ceased; King Ibn Saud of Saudi Arabia and King Faisal of Iraq had settled their differences and reached a state of uneasy peace, but these rulers had little control over the Bedouin tribesmen, for whom in any case, raiding and pillage was a way of life, with trading caravans providing easy pickings. Moreover, the influence of Allah and the Koran were much stronger than that of a ruler in some remote capital, consequently the luckless infidel pilot of a forced-down aircraft seldom survived unless he was quickly found and rescued by a combined air and armoured car search party.

In theory a captive could save his life if he seized the hem of the jelaba worn by the most influential-looking tribesman and shouted the word 'daheel' (mercy). The person thus addressed must then, by tribal custom and Muslim etiquette, protect the life of the captive, even at risk of his own life, but though you might save your skin the end result would be little better than death. Despised of all men, you would become and remain a slave to your protector.

If a forced-landed or crashed aircraft, when found, was partially or wholly salvageable—and it was seldom possible because of transport difficulties to recover anything more than the engine, instruments and guns and ammunition, always supposing that the

Bedouin hadn't already helped themselves to the latter—it called for a major expedition, as the following description illustrates.

A twin-engined aircraft had crashed in the desert about seventy-five miles from the nearest form of normal transport. The necessary salvage equipment was conveyed in two convoys each of ten camels.

Special trotting camels were provided for Royal Air Force personnel.

Tool kits, water and rations were carried by the remaining camels on the outward journey. The total weight, including the human load, was about 4500lb and the loads carried by individual camels on the return journey were disposed as follows:

Twelve engine cylinders packed in native cloth and slung six on either side, plus hand starting gear and water pipes on the animal's back.

Crankshaft and epicyclic gear wrapped in sacking and slung by ropes at each crank pin, with the crankcase slung on the other side to balance the load.

Wheels slung two on either side, with a packing of dried shrubs to prevent chafing.

Engine sumps slung one on either side, with electrical fittings, control levers and the bombsight hung over the sumps.

Parachutes and bomb racks, guns and ammunition packed in bags and disposed on either side.

Twenty-four pistons and connecting rods in bags, twelve per side.

Instruments packed in scrub and camel thorn, and two cam-shafts on one side balanced by pumps and dynamos on the other.

Other items were suitably disposed among the remaining camels, together with spare kit, fitters and riggers tools, water, food, bedding, tents, cooking gear and camel fodder.

The average load for a camel is 350lb and this includes a driver, on the basis of one man having charge of two camels.

Progress is slow. A trotting camel can average seven miles an hour and can cover twenty-five miles in a day. A pack camel can manage fifteen to eighteen miles a day, moving at one and a half to two miles an hour.

A camel endures thirst, hunger and pain better than any other animal, but dislikes changes of climate, and if you are ever faced with a long journey by camel, remember that marching should be done at the coolest part of the day and grazing during the hottest; also that the camel requires six hours a day to feed and prefers still water to running water—which is fortunate, since there is seldom anything else.

In passing, the daily ration for Bedouin camel drivers and labourers, as approved and sanctioned by the Royal Air Force, was:

<table>
<tr><td>*Native bread 2lb*</td><td>*Onions 4oz*</td></tr>
<tr><td>*Meat 3oz*</td><td>*Salt ⅛oz*</td></tr>
<tr><td>*Lentils or beans 4oz*</td><td>*Cooking oil 1oz*</td></tr>
<tr><td>*Rice 2oz*</td><td></td></tr>
</table>

By contrast, British daily field ration (though I hasten to add not on an expedition such as the foregoing where weight had to be kept to a minimum) was:

<table>
<tr><td>*1lb fresh or frozen meat, or 12oz (1 can) bully beef*</td><td>*1½oz condensed milk*</td></tr>
<tr><td>*1lb bread or 12oz biscuit or 12oz flour*</td><td>*⅝oz tea*
3oz sugar</td></tr>
<tr><td>*3oz bacon*</td><td>*¼oz salt*</td></tr>
<tr><td>*2oz cheese*</td><td>*1/100oz each of mustard and pepper*</td></tr>
<tr><td>*12oz fresh vegetables or fresh fruit or dried peas and beans*</td><td>*½ gill rum*</td></tr>
<tr><td>*2oz jam*</td><td>*1/10 gill lemon or lime juice*</td></tr>
<tr><td>*1oz butter or margarine*</td><td>*2oz tobacco a week.*</td></tr>
</table>

We were not really hard done by.

However, things were anything but quiet in the mountain territories of Kurdistan. Racially Kurdistan was not unlike Lapland. The Laps, though one people, are split territorially between Norway, Sweden and Finland. The Kurds, also one people, were split territorially between Turkey, Persia and Iraq, and of the three they hated the Iraqi Arabs the most.

Their powerful Shaikh Mahmoud had been a thorn in the side of the mandatory power and of Baghdad since the defeat of the Turks and still was, so that although throughout my time in Iraq we never fired a shot in anger in the desert, we were kept very busy in the hill country.

The squadron returned to Hinaidi and it became necessary to learn to be a fully operational pilot. At Abu Sueir you had been taught to fly an aeroplane to the point where you could be let loose in it without immediate peril to yourself and everyone else. It was the squadron's job to teach everything else: formation flying and night flying; front and rear gunnery; high level, medium and low level bombing, singly and in formation; dive bombing; and doing your stint in the rear cockpit as gunner and bomb-aimer, using the Wimperis bomb sight, so that you would be cognisant of the problems with which the gunner had to contend and would therefore know how the aeroplane ought to be flown to give him the best possible conditions. You were taught about aerial photography, low-altitude oblique and high-altitude vertical, and about how to carry out a reconnaissance, put the correct interpretation on what you saw and write a reconnaissance report.

You learned for example that the Bedouin rode camels and had no livestock, except perhaps for a few sheep, but that if you saw horsemen they were nomads and if on migration would have a lot of sheep.

You learned to tell by the colour of the jelaba and shafia (headgear) whether the Bedouin were Akhwan or Wahabi (Ibn Saud's men), and whether they were a raiding party or peaceful. If they were peaceful (for the moment) their banners would be furled and would look like lances. If they were in a large body of several thousand, and accompanied by women, livestock and unridden animals, that would be loot after a successful raid. You were taught how to survive in the desert and the hills and how, in theory at any rate, to save your own skin if captured.

You had to know the subtle differences between the Muslim sects: why what was acceptable to a Shia Muslim might be anathema to a Sunni, why it was an insult when a guest to let the soles of your feet point towards your host, and why it was unclean to eat or touch food with the left hand. You learnt that you must never allow your infidel shadow to fall upon a Muslim at prayer, and to understand that in Bedouin company mention of women, dogs and pigs was absolutely taboo.

Etiquette and customs of the service were child's play compared with etiquette and customs of the tribesmen. There was a lot to learn, but first we had to get used to flying the new Wapitis. However, before leaving the old DH9A for ever, I should like to mention that an occasional drawback to flying them in Iraq was the liquid-cooled engine in a locust year. It is difficult to describe the impressive horror of a plague of locusts. They did not come in thousands, but in millions or even billions. The air would be thick with them, advancing along a broad front a quarter of a mile across and towering from ground level up to one or two hundred feet. The column stretched from horizon to horizon and its passing, if indeed they were passing and not settling, could take all day or several days.

If you taxied out and took off, as you often had to, in this cloud of heavy-bodied four-inch-long insects, the radiator became completely clogged and useless, so you took off without delay with the radiator shutters closed.

The engine boiled before you got off the ground, but you hoped to have time to climb through the locusts into clear air and open the shutters before it seized up.

The Wapiti was not affected. The cooling fins on the big air-cooled radial would clog up, but the insects were quickly incinerated so that you only got a very brief period of overheating.

CHAPTER 4

As the Ninak grew out of the DH4, so in a sense was the Wapiti whelped by the 9A, a replacement for which was long overdue; when this requirement was made known by Air Ministry the Treasury, with typical (some might say commendable) parsimony, ruled that any such replacement must be designed and built in a way that would enable it to utilise the thousands of 9A spares lying about in squadrons and depots, particularly overseas.

A specification No 26/27 was drawn up and manufacturers invited to submit entries and tenders. A preference was expressed for all-metal structures. Eight designs were offered: the Armstrong Whitworth Atlas, the Bristol Beaver, the De Havilland Stag, the Gloster Goral, the Fairey IIIF, the Vickers Valiant and Vickers Vixen and the Westland Wapiti.

Westlands, having built all the DH9As, were well able to design an aircraft capable of using up 9A spares, but in fact only the prototype was built incorporating 9A components, of which the wings, ailerons, interplane struts and tail surfaces alone were used. The fuselage, employing a new concept of all-metal construction, was wider and deeper than that of the old 9A.

This prototype Wapiti, after acceptance trials, flew in the 1927 RAF display at Hendon. Only the first twenty-five aircraft, designated Mk I, were of wooden construction and these had the Bristol Jupiter VI ungeared engine of 420hp. There followed the Mk II, to specification 16/31, and then the Mk IIA, which was the first all-metal version and had the geared Jupiter VIIIF engine of 480hp.

Iraq was the first command to be equipped with the type, 84 squadron getting theirs in 1928, followed by 30 squadron. 55 did not re-equip until early 1930, which is where I came into the picture.

They were good-looking aeroplanes and nice to fly; we liked them. They were not fully aerobatic but could be spun, looped and stall turned. However, even that modest repertoire was hard on the rear cockpit occupant, who had no Sutton harness, only a wire cable attached to a ringbolt on the floor which he could clip to his parachute harness by means of a snap swivel; unless he hung on like grim death with both hands he would, in inverted flight such as at the top of a badly executed loop, fall out and dangle on the end of his cable.

The Wapiti had an oleo leg undercarriage and was easier to land than the 9A. There was a gated throttle to provide maximum power for take off or emergency and a nice stick with a spade grip and a neat thumb-operated front gun button. Apart from a cross level and a cylinder-head temperature gauge, instruments were no more sophisticated than on the 9A or Avro. Performance was what you would expect in the early thirties: cruising speed 100–110mph; maximum 140mph; stalling speed 56mph; service ceiling 20,600ft; range 530 miles.

There was no shortage of good experienced pilots in the squadron to show the new boy how it should be done. The CO and all three flight commanders had seen service in the Great War and my first flight commander, Dollie Gray, was a former Martlesham Heath test pilot.

Formation flying was the first thing to learn. A flight is not a flight, nor a squadron a squadron, if it cannot fly good formation; 55 was reckoned to be about the best there was and was always ready to demonstrate the fact.

There was no dual instruction; you took off, caught up with the leader as best you could and tried to stay with him, slithering about too fast or too slow, slipping in or skidding out on the turns, sliding sideways past his tail, or by over-correcting fore and aft getting above and losing sight of him altogether. How he could just sit there apparently unmoved, in imminent danger of having some ass (me) cut his tail off with a bloody great prop, was deserving of the greatest admiration, but we all have to learn, and one day my turn would come to sit there calmly whilst some other idiot cut his formation flying teeth, so to speak, on my tail plane.

The squadron's pride in its formation flying was not all swank. The tighter the aircraft tuck into each other, except in very bumpy conditions, the easier the flight or squadron is to control. The leader must be able to fly the formation as though it were one aircraft. This was especially true for the low performance aircraft of the early days. In a widely-spaced formation, with only about 60mph between stalling and flat out, the inside aircraft of a squadron of nine during a turn might stall and drop out while the outside one would have insufficient speed to keep up. All errors of station-keeping are magnified for the next aircraft. Thus if number 2, that is the pilot flying next to and to starboard of the leader, over-corrects or flies sloppily, by the time his error works through to number 8 on the outer edge of the starboard echelon, he, poor chap, will be thrashing about like a whip.

The insistence on good formation flying was not an end in itself. For example, in a squadron bombing exercise, whether for practice or for real, the closer the formation the tighter the bomb pattern.

Which reminds me of the time we bombed the AOC-in-C. By then I had become an old hand (two whole years service). Every year culminated in the dreaded AOC's inspection, which was not just a cursory look round a bulled-up station and a spit and polish parade. It went on for days and included all aspects of flying and ground work.

At this time, because of postings and illness and people killing themselves I had become, though only a very junior Flying Officer, flight commander of 'B' flight. It also happened that, thanks entirely to Corporal Bailey, I had obtained the best results in the individual bombing classification; hence I was chosen to lead the squadron on the bombing exercise for the old man, which was to be with live bombs, the 20lb Coopers.

Regrettably, our squadron commander had told the AOC how good we were and that there was no need to watch from right back in the safety of the Vector hut. It would be all right, he said, if the air marshal and his staff stationed themselves much closer to the

Top: No. 4 FTS, Abu Sueir, Egypt.

Above: Smoke candle to indicate wind speed and direction.

Vickers Vimy Bomber;
2 Rolls-Royce Eagle engines.
Service type trainer for the
ham fisted.

A Hucks starter driven by
sprocket and chain from the
transmission of a Model T
Ford.

Top Left: The DH9A's could stand well on their big flat noses.

Left: Flying instructors were quite capable of breaking aeroplanes without any help from beginners. A Flight Commander killed himself and his pupil in this one.

Top: Though less spectacular, it is better not to land your DH9A on someone else's.

Above: Refuelling a Gloster Grebe from 4-gallon cans. This little SS fighter was exclusively for use by instructors.

Above: With Padre Warner, later Dean of Lincoln, halfway through the course. We are now down to thirteen, having started with twenty-two. Two of these went before the end.

Left: Squadron Leaders with their boots on: Charles Roderick Carr, Chief Flying Instructor, 4 FTS.

Right: Proud moment. The author has just completed final passing-out test with the Chief Flying Instructor. Time, winter. Tropical radiator blanked off.

Top Left: Baghdad. No longer mirage. New street carved straight through the centre of Haroun Al Rashid's city by the British Army in the 1914–18 War.

Far Left: An operational DH9A. Note front and rear guns, bomb racks, screw pickets lashed to wing tip skids, and thing for carrying things in. The tank under the starboard upper mainplane holds 40 gallons of drinking water just in case. The crew are wearing 'Baghdad bowlers'—aviation topees.

Above: The Arch of Ctesiphon, former palace of the Sassanid Dynasty, AD224–641. The Squadron's bombing and gunnery ranges were close by, and good sand grouse shooting too.

Left: Busaihia Fort in the southern desert. We got there by the grace of Allah, who was ably assisted by Corporal Bailey.

Above: North West Frontier version of the Goli Chit.

Top Right: Vickers Victoria of 70 Squadron, as used in the evacuation of Kabul.

Right: Akhwan tribesman. His wife will cut 'em out for you with the skill born of long practice.

Above: We thought we knew a thing or two about formation flying. These are the aircraft which nearly came to grief when they collided with the ducks over the Baquba marshes.

Top Right: King Ibn Saud of Saudi Arabia, King Faisal of Iraq and Sir Francis Humphreys, High Commissioner for Iraq, on board a navy frigate in the Shatt Al Arab. They settled their differences.

Right: A Wapiti of 'A' Flight. The colour scheme was: 'A' Flight, red top decking, red lettering and red squadron crest; 'B' Flight, blue; 'C' Flight, black with a broken white line. Note the mounting for wing tip flares below the front outer interplane struts.

Top: A chap named Chichester arrived in a DH Moth. He said he was flying to Australia.

Top Right: In tropical mess kit, the junior officers of 55 Squadron.

Bottom: A very good argument for not using both wing tip flares when doing a night landing.

Far Right: The author and two Waler/Arab crosses.

Above: The Delage and
shooting party. Ascari, author.
Friday and 'Tubby' Earl,
later Air Marshal Sir A.

Left: 2 guns, 3 beaters, 1
bodyguard.

target. We had after all just yesterday achieved from 10,000 feet a bombing error of only ten yards from the centre of the target.

The AOC's staff car was a white Rolls Royce open tourer, which stood out like a sore thumb even from 10,000 feet. I don't know what went wrong that day. It could be that I, or Corporal B, the bomb-aimer, mistook the Rolls for the target—a white cross. Or, what is more likely, we had applied the wrong wind to the Wimperis bomb sight. In those days there was no question of telephoning the Met. Office for the upper winds. They had no way of finding out, so if you needed to know the wind speed and direction at 10,000 feet you had to engage in some do-it-yourself meteorology, by the triangle of velocities method in which you flew three separate headings, differing from each other by 120°, over a given pinpoint, in this case the target, for a given number of minutes at a constant airspeed. Anyhow, the bombing error was 150 yards instead of ten. That would not have mattered much had it been undershoot or overshoot, but it wasn't; it was to starboard, slap between the target and the Vector hut. We couldn't see the confusion from 10,000 feet, but I gather the exalted party ran for their lives, leaving the Rolls to its fate. No one was hurt, but the old man wasn't impressed and any hope the CO might have entertained of quick promotion to Wing Commander was forlorn.

Air to ground gunnery and dive bombing was great fun. For the gunnery a shallow dive was best, because you had the target for a much longer period and could get in four or five good bursts starting from about 400 yards. As you pulled up, having passed the target, the rear gunner opened up with the Lewis.

It was the general practice to combine dive bombing, using the 20lb fragmentation Cooper bombs, with the gunnery, but I found the two together lacked accuracy for one or the other. For the bombing a steep dive was more effective, but the speed built up too quickly if you merely shoved the stick forward from straight and level. The better way was to make two distinct attacks. Guns first, then climb steeply on full power and stall turn on to the target for the bombing run, coming in from a different direction on each attack.

Night flying presented the greatest hazards, not because it is particularly difficult or very different from flying in daylight, but because the aids were so primitive.

There was no dual instruction aircraft in the squadron. You

merely took a back seat ride with an experienced pilot and then got into the cockpit and tried your luck in ballast at first, but after three successful circuits and landings you took your air gunner.

The signalling system was simple enough. In addition to the navigation lights, red to port, green to starboard and white astern, the aircraft carried white upward and downward recognition lights.

When you were ready to taxi out, you flashed your morse code call sign on the recognition lights and when you got a green on the Aldis lamp from the officer i/c flare path, you taxied out, lined up with the flares and took off.

For landing there was the same system of signalling, leaving your recognition lights on when you got the green affirmative. If you got a red, you acknowledged by flashing the recognition lights and stooged around until the wreckage of the last to land had been cleared away.

The flare path was a collection of paraffin flares laid out in the form of a T. Naturally, the officer in charge of night flying was known as Paraffin Pete. The object was not so much to provide illumination by which to see the ground, more a datum by which, as the angle changed and the T became foreshortened, you could judge the right moment to round out the approach and—you hoped —put the aeroplane neatly and tidily on to the ground.

The aircraft were also fitted with wing-tip flares. These fearsome pyrotechnics, detonated electrically, were supposed to provide enough illumination to show you where the ground was, provided you were already down to about 50 or 100 feet. They were of marginal value only and intended for emergency, and no one in his right mind used them when he had a flare path. If you did use them it was essential to light only one, the one opposite the side you habitually looked out of when landing. If, as most pilots in single-engined open cockpit aeroplanes did, you looked out along the port engine cowling then you would light the starboard flare, and even that gave such a terrific back glare from the spinning disc of the airscrew that you could see almost nothing.

One night about half way through my tour of duty, a new squadron commander, whom we had acquired straight from a desk at Air Ministry, decided to show the squadron how it should be done. He announced his intention of landing with both wing tip flares burning. We all tried desperately to dissuade him, but to no avail. "Rubbish," he said, "you are talking balls," and off he went. In due course in he came, fired both flares at about 400 feet, and quite obviously from there on could see nothing.

He did not hold off at all but flew straight into the ground, wiped off the undercarriage and of course caught fire, but stepped out without a scratch.

Less fortunate was the CO of our sister squadron, number 84 down at Shaibah. He, Squadron Leader Stewart, did precisely the same thing a month later and killed himself and his airgunner.

That same CO (ours, not 84 squadron's) was quite the worst pilot imaginable, but he was full of guts and we liked him. He had begun his military career as a trooper in a cavalry regiment, becoming a rough-riding instructor. During the 1914–18 war he had transferred to the RFC, learned to fly and was commissioned. This was his second tour of duty in Iraq.

His first was back in 1922 when the desert wars were at their fiercest. Shot down in the desert, he was captured by the Akhwan and at the hands of the women suffered the fate we all joked about but secretly dreaded. Left for dead, he not only survived castration —few men do, at any rate among those who are victims of Bedouin surgical practitioners—but somehow escaped and got back to the British lines. I used often to visit him in later years at his home in the South of England and gradually got the whole story from him. The tribeswomen did a clumsy job and the remains of the second one were removed in less brutal circumstances in England. However, he was in more or less constant pain throughout his life after 1922.

He had a sweet gentle wife and it was their joint tragedy and sorrow that they were unable to have a family. It is true about the squeaky voice; he had one, and not surprisingly hated all Arabs with a deep and bitter loathing.

On one occasion he lost the entire squadron, which he was leading on a flight from Baghdad to Amman in Jordan. The weather en route deteriorated to gale force winds and sand storms. It was quite impossible to maintain formation and indeed highly dangerous to try. The squadron became lost and scattered all over the desert. Of the nine aircraft which set out, seven crashed. GC had an absolute fixation about formation flying. Wing-tip to wing-tip stuff was all right for children and fighter boys. *His* squadron had to fly wing-tip to cockpit, tucked right in and overlapping. To this end he had a platform built over the rear cockpit of his aircraft on which, with Hamish Mahaddie doing the flying, he could kneel facing aft, from which position he controlled the formation with hand signals, waving the formating pilots ever closer. He was only satisfied when he was able to stretch out his arms and grasp the wing-tips of numbers one and three. If he was short of a round object or two, he was certainly not short of guts.

Formation flying of such precision had no direct military application but was good for morale. It demanded intense concentration and microsecond reactions. You never took your eyes off the leader, so there was no question of being able to refer to instruments. In still air it was quite easy, but in rough conditions you had your work cut out to keep station, playing the throttle like a musical instrument and the stick like a madman stirring porridge. It was not an exercise for novices nor was it to be recommended for those with a hangover. You needed to be bright-eyed and bushy-tailed.

The entire service was full of characters, of which 55 certainly had its share.

There was Bertie, who had wangled a posting overseas to escape his creditors. A story was told of his experience at a home station, where the flight sergeant of his flight was well aware of Bertie's financial difficulties. He marched into the flight office one day, saluted smartly and said, "Mr. X, sir, there's a man in a bowler 'at outside. I've started your machine up."

There was Marmaduke, also with acute financial problems, so much so that all his pay and allowances were ordered to be handed over to the adjutant, who paid the bills and doled out to Marmaduke five pounds a month pocket money. He eventually left the service under a bit of a cloud, but gallantly rejoined as a sergeant pilot at the beginning of the war and was killed on active service when the wings fell off the Miles Master he was flying.

Rudolph T, flight commander of 'C' flight, was a hard-riding, hard-drinking, polo-playing Irishman, who captained the squadron polo team and taught us all to play.

Polo was popular at Hinaidi and cheap. There was a thing called the AOC's Sports Fund from which an impecunious junior officer could borrow the purchase price of two polo ponies and repay it so much a month on his mess bill. The minimum requirement if you meant to play polo seriously was three ponies, plus one Iraq cavalry animal on loan from the remount depot. The ponies were

52

Walers, that is, Australian stock ponies left behind by the Indian Army, or pure bred Arabs purchased from the desert Shaikhs. Your first mount essentially had to be a 'made' polo pony from whom, with the help of Rudolph, you learned the game. This one you usually bought from the chap you were relieving, at a cost of 600 to 1,000 rupees. The other two you bought unbroken from the Bedouin, for about 150 rupees each (£12). Feed and stabling came to £3 a month and you shared a syce (groom) with a brother officer. The syce's wages were £5 a month. Membership of the Gymkhana Club was three guineas a year. It is unlikely that, even in India, polo could be any cheaper than that.

There was also the Exodus hunt, with a good pack of hounds built up from a few original couples brought out from the Meynell. We hunted jackal, so it wouldn't have done for the Quorn.

The MO was quite a chap too; also Irish, he had learned his trade at Trinity, Dublin. One night at a party with 84 squadron, when he had already had a fair amount to drink, he undertook to drink a bottle of gin at one go. He did, and as the last drops trickled down his throat he fell flat on his back and was unconscious for two days.

But the larger-than-life character to end all characters was undoubtedly 'Hunker', flight commander of 'A' flight. Not for nothing was he called Hunker; a huge man with an infinite capacity for hard liquor, he had been with number 1 fighter squadron, but when they returned to England had chosen to stay on in Iraq with a posting to 55.

He had retained the same Madrasi servant the whole time and would not go anywhere without him, nor would the man be left behind. To anyone else this could have presented a problem when a squadron of single-seater fighters went up country on detachment, but not to Hunker. He used to have the man lashed to the lower main plane, hard up against the fuselage, and fly him to wherever they might be going. The Snipe had the Bentley rotary engine, so inevitably the wretched servant would reach journey's end covered from head to foot in castor oil.

Not just the man himself, but everything connected with Hunker was larger than life, including his flight sergeant in 'A' flight. This could only have been fortuitous. He could not possibly have picked him specially out of all the flight sergeants in the service.

Flight Sergeant Barleycorn ought to have been a butler. Perhaps he *had* been a butler. He certainly exhibited all the hallmarks of that admirable breed.

They treated each other with the utmost decorum and an air of old-world courtesy and formality. For example, when Hunker at the end of the working day—1100 hours—was ready to state his requirements for the morrow, he would say, "Flight sergeant, I shall want four aircraft tomorrow morning. My purpose holds to exercise the young gentlemen in the art of formation flying. The commanding officer has expressed the opinion that our performance in this respect yesterday fell short of the standard he has come to expect."

"Very good, sir," says Barleycorn. "That will be yourself, sir, in A1, sir. Mr. Thursday, sir, in A2, sir. Flying on your right, sir. Mr. Prune, sir, flying A3, sir, on your left, sir, and Sergeant Keen, sir, in A5, sir, flying astern, sir." Hunker would listen to this long-winded rigmarole with stoic calm. "Excellent, flight sergeant, excellent, but why may I ask is the reserve aircraft A5 to be flown?"

"I regret to inform you, sir, that A4 is unserviceable, sir. Mr. Crump, sir, made a heavy landing, sir." "Then I shall speak to that young man."

"Indeed, sir, that would be most salutary."

Flight Sergeant Barleycorn hated flying, yet occasionally, and with uncharacteristic sadism, Hunker would invite him to occupy the rear cockpit. Barleycorn never got the hang of handling a parachute. The troops in the flight knew it and made the most of it. Barleycorn said that when he was in the Royal Engineers on Laffans Plain, Colonel Cody's aeroplanes didn't even have engines, let alone new-fangled fol de rols like parachutes. The service was getting soft. Going to the dogs.

The passenger, or crew member, had the lap type parachute. He wore the harness but stowed the pack in the cockpit, well out **of** the way, where it would not impede free movement. As everyone knows, the lap pack has a ring on either side by which it is attached to the harness.

The troops would help Barleycorn into the harness, as often as not back to front; then, carefully manoeuvring him to ensure that he was standing in the slipstream, they would hand him the pack in such a manner that the obvious and only way to take it was by the 'D' ring of the ripcord.

They would then let go suddenly and of course the weight of

the pack would pull the ripcord, and there the poor old flight sergeant would be, with an open chute and the canopy billowing out nicely in the slipstream.

It happened every time.

When the squadron was on operations in Kurdistan, Barleycorn would appear at the flap of Hunker's tent, salute smartly and announce with all solemnity, "Dawn is breaking, sir." Hunker would invariably say, "Thank you, flight sergeant, but kindly prevail upon the Almighty to stick it together again. I'm not ready." Without a glimmer of a smile, Barleycorn would salute, say "Very good, sir," and disappear for ten minutes, only to repeat the ritual all over again.

Weeks would go by with Hunker on the wagon, but every so often he would break out. One such occasion came at a time when the squadron was without a CO and Hunker, being the senior flight lieutenant, was in command. By this time I was the senior flying officer in 'B' flight and thus acting as flight commander.

At 4.30 one morning all the squadron's aircraft were lined up on the tarmac ticking over. Along came Hunker, having without warning started one of his periodical benders the night before.

"What are all these aeroplanes doing?" he demanded.

"About to take off, sir, air to ground gunnery."

"Put 'em all away," he said, "the day will be devoted to drinking."

It was an order, but unfortunately it didn't stop at one day. This one went on for the best part of a week, during which the entire mess was wholly or partially paralytic, and Hunker only just escaped court martial on a charge of 'conduct unbecoming an Officer and Gentleman'. Alternative charge: 'conduct to the prejudice of good order and Air Force discipline'.

A junior officer's wine bill was limited to £5 per month. If he exceeded this amount he was instructed to report to the CO and invited to explain himself. In fact, it was a more than generous allowance. Gordon's gin was 1/6d a bottle, whisky 2/6d, Johnny Walker Black Label 3/–. Beer was the most expensive drink there was. As for cigarettes, Players Navy Cut in sealed tins of 50 cost 1/3d. In the mess, gin or whisky by the tot was 2d.

Often we would roar into Baghdad to dine at the Maude. In hot weather dinner for the Sahibs was always served on the terrace, which jutted out over the Tigris—an invitation to disaster.

The cuisine was limited. The grilled black partridge or sand-grouse, when in season, were excellent, as were the curries, but the steaks were terrible, being cut from the rear end of a water buffalo too old to go on working; but good or bad, if Hunker disapproved he would throw first his own into the river, then everybody else's, and since cutlery was useless without food, that too would be flung into the Tigris; next all the glasses, then the tables and finally the chairs. At this point the waiters would cease to protest and disappear at speed—they knew from bitter experience whose turn was next. The proprietor loved it; all he had to do was to send in a bill for five times what the stuff was worth, knowing he would always be paid.

It was all incredibly juvenile, but it seemed funny at the time, as did everything else.

Like the leg-pulling to which Alfie was permanently subjected. Alfie was a good-natured long-suffering Yorkshireman, who sounded like a north-country comedian. Only once did he lose his temper, and then only to shout, "I joined t'Royal Air Force to get a soothern accent, and all that 'appens is you silly boogers go and talk laik me."

McEvoy had joined the Squadron by this time, having transferred from the aircraft depot on choosing to serve an extra year in Iraq, and was commanding the flight to which both Marmaduke and Alfie belonged.

Rather late one night Marmaduke felt impelled to go out after a jackal with his .410 shot gun and Mac, as his flight commander, decided to go with him. On the way they thought it would be a good idea to get Alfie out of bed; which they did, but unfortunately the gun was loaded. Alfie got peppered, for which they were both court-martialled; Marmaduke because he had done the shooting, and Mac because he was the senior officer present. Alfie bore nobody any ill-will.

One thing, during these partying sessions, stood out like a beacon. No one was ever late for a parade or failed to be ready for the dawn take-off (except during Hunker's lost week). My own method, knowing the risk of not waking up at four though having only got to bed at two, was to return to quarters, shave and shower, get into khaki shirt and shorts, go down to the hangars, climb into the cockpit of my aircraft and fall fast asleep right there. You couldn't fail to be on the job. When the troops pushed the aircraft out in the half-light of the desert dawn there you were, bleary-eyed but ready to go.

To talk of taking a shower is praising it. Sanitation was primitive and plumbing non-existent. The ubiquitous four-gallon petrol can served many purposes. Cut in half lengthwise and placed one under each seat in the bogs, they pre-dated the Elsan by several years. With holes punched in the top, rigged up on a sort of bell crank and kept filled with water by your servant, they served as a shower; you stood underneath and pulled a cord, which turned it upside down and gave you a fine wetting.

Cut open and flattened, the wogs used them to line the walls and flat roofs of their mud huts.

Sunday morning was the time you visited the other messes, 70 squadron, the Depot, or the armoured car boys. There was a ritual which hardly varied. Mercifully, compulsory church parade in the garrison church was only once a month, since it couldn't hold everyone; so most Sundays allowed time for recovery from Saturday night's hangover.

The ritual was the war of the insects. Most people have a horror of the nastier creepy-crawlies and this was perhaps our way of getting even. In each squadron there was always someone who had one or more captive tarantulas, centipedes or scorpions, or maybe all three. All of them were horrid and could be deadly, but the ones that still make me shudder were the centipedes. Not your nice harmless little English garden centipedes, but ghastly great poisonous desert monsters five inches long and half an inch wide, with a hard dirty-yellow shell and a chocolate-brown streak down the back. If you were unlucky enough to find one crawling up an arm or leg, it was imperative to brush it off the way it was walking. Instinctively you would want to brush it off the other way, which was fatal. All its feet would dig into your flesh and break off, and each puncture would turn septic.

At these Sunday morning contests we would bet on A's scorpion beating B's tarantula, or C's centipede beating both. The creatures were put into one of those enormous shallow copper bowls that the Arabs used for practically everything. They couldn't climb out, since the sides were shiny and just too steep, so they fought each other instead. Generally a scorpion would kill a tarantula, though not always, but the centipede always won. They moved like lightning and knew exactly where the scorpion's armoury was.

The centipede would bide his time, evading the attacks of the scorpion, then suddenly, almost too quick to see, it would have half its legs wrapped around the scorpion's tail, rendering it harmless, bite into the soft underbelly of the scorpion and just go on eating. If you think it was cruel, consider the fate of the sergeant who, all innocent and contemplative, sat communing with nature poised above one of the aforementioned half petrol cans, and was stung on the goolies by a scorpion. It killed him. True, he should have looked before he sat, but he might have been in a hurry.

It is not for nothing that 84 squadron has for its squadron crest a scorpion rampant.

Shaibah was the desert station to end all desert stations: a small collection of World War I huts and Bessoneau hangars, ringed by barbed wire and surrounded by miles and miles of nothing—not a tree, not a blade of grass, just sand and camel thorn. 'Shaibah Blues'—the troops had a song about it, a dirge to the tune of 'A little bit of heaven fell from out the sky one day' with the words:

> A little bit of Muttie fell from out the sky one day
> And it landed down at Shaibah many thousand miles away
> And when Lord Trenchard saw it, sure it looked so grim and
> bare,
> He said, "that's what I'm looking for, we'll put our Air Force
> there."

How that man Trenchard dominated everyone's thoughts! There was another song in which he featured, a plagiarised version of the children's hymn 'Jesus loves us'. It will not bear repetition.

The summer temperature all over Iraq is pretty torrid. In the central area, including Hinaidi, it was 120–130° in the shade at mid-day, but at least it was a dry heat and thus bearable. Down at Shaibah it could rise to 140°, with high humidity. During the day it was not possible to do anything except lie on your bunk with a towel round your middle, right underneath the electric punkah.

All the troopships had a padded cell in the forepeak. They seldom had less than five occupants on every ship returning to the UK. Of the five at least two would be from Shaibah.

The damnedest things happened at Shaibah (quite apart from the squadron commander killing himself night flying).

One hot oppressive afternoon, when most people were having

their post-luncheon siesta, one of the officers suddenly went mad; at least it *seemed* sudden, though no doubt it had been coming on for a long time, but in an environment where everybody was a bit odd at one time or another (save thee and me) it would not have been remarkable enough to attract attention.

Anyhow he, so the report went, rushed out of his quarter stark naked and into the mess kitchen, where he seized a large butcher's knife and then set off for the adjutant's quarter, obviously with the intention of doing him a grave disservice (I wonder why it's always the poor bloody adjutant?).

The adjutant, also stark naked—everybody always was at that time of day, since clothes of any sort were quite insupportable—after running round and round the bed managed to get out through the door and, with the other in hot—and it would be all of that—pursuit, fled toward the tennis court, which with its eight-foot perimeter fence and only the one gate must have seemed like a safe haven.

However, in his haste he neglected to shut and bolt the gate, so he was now in fact worse off, being cornered with no other exit. Fortunately his frenzied shouts for help were heard and his adversary was overpowered by sheer weight of numbers, just in time.

And thus another candidate for the padded cell in the next troopship bound for UK.

Then there was the airman who shot himself with his service .303 Lee Enfield. He too must have given it a lot of thought because his careful and precise preparations could not have been completed except over a long period, especially when you consider how very little private life the troops had and how seldom they would be alone in their barrack huts. He was not a skilled fitter for nothing; what he had done was to make a cradle and clamp to fit over the foot of his bed, and had then designed a system of pulleys over which to pass a stout cord. When all was to his satisfaction, and he must have had several dummy runs to get it right, he got on to his bed, propping himself up so that he would be looking straight down the muzzle, then with his big toe thrust through a loop in the end of the cord pulled the trigger. It was a really neat craftsman's job.

As if that wasn't enough, all four of the Indian cooks in the officers' mess managed to burn themselves to death, in most tragic circumstances, just because they were trying to do a good job.

The kitchen floor was of concrete and had over the years become caked with grease and dirt. With the primitive cleaning gear of those days, consisting of metal scrapers followed by scrubbing brushes and soap—no detergent—it was not easy to keep clean.

They knew about the cleaning properties of petrol, so went and stole some from the MT section, and not wanting to be caught, chose a time—mid-afternoon—when everybody would be sleeping and locked themselves in.

The rest is deduction. Presumably they sloshed the petrol on to the floor, whereupon it promptly ran, as it usually does, all over the place, some of it finally reaching the hot stoves, where it flash exploded.

The services in Iraq were an all-male society. Wives and families were not allowed. It was a monk-like existence. There was no such thing as airmen's welfare, nor officers' either for that matter. You made your own fun, which wasn't all that difficult.

An overseas tour of duty was five years in all commands, except for Iraq and Aden, where it was two. This was fine for officers, who after completing their two years could opt for a posting home. Not so, however, for NCOs and other ranks, who had to do a full five years come what may; so if they did the first two in Iraq, they would be posted either to Egypt, Palestine, Transjordan or India for the last three. So, once a year, a draft of men would be sent to India. The job of shepherding this lot generally fell to the most junior officer in the squadron, which is how I came to the brink of court martial.

I was detailed to conduct a draft of 100 NCOs and airmen to Kohat in the North West Frontier Province, and we left Baghdad for Basrah on that terrible railway built by the Turks just before the Great War.

It was insufferably hot and sticky, and everything which was not covered in sand and dust was black with flies. The train journey was going to be two days of hell and the only advice tendered was "drink yourself into a stupor, old boy, and you won't notice".

At Basrah we boarded a troopship outward bound from UK, the good ship *Devonshire* of the British India Line. If you haven't travelled by troopship, you haven't lived. The officers' quarters and messes were tolerable and about comparable with second-class travel in a P & O, but the troops' decks were a disgrace and the

60

soldiers' and airmen's married families' accommodation incredibly insanitary. Conditions could not have been a lot worse in the slavers of a bygone age.

We docked at Karachi around tea time. My orders were to get the troops entrained for the journey across the Sind desert to Kohat at 0900 hours the following day. The senior NCO came to my cabin.

"Sir, permission to speak, sir?"

"Yes, flight sergeant."

"Can the men have shore leave please, sir?"

Well, why not. It was hot and sticky on board and they had been cooped up for a long time.

"Very well, flight sergeant, eight-hour passes for everyone; get the passes made out and I'll sign them; back on board before midnight."

In no time the whole bunch were climbing into gharries and away. The NCOs had already got it laid on. A green young pilot officer is no match for a tough old senior NCO when it comes to a bit of low cunning.

Next morning, at what should have been roll-call, look—no troops. I wasn't left long in doubt. Would Mr. Carr—you were always mister until you reached the dizzy rank of flight lieutenant —kindly step along to the captain's day cabin? Someone from the Provost Marshal's office had come aboard.

"You are in trouble, laddie. All your men were picked up by the MPs in the red light district last night and are in the cooler. There is to be a court of enquiry; I wouldn't be you for a big gold clock."

Signals flashed around the world. C in C India to C in C Iraq, C in C Iraq to Air Ministry, London. What shall we do with this misbegotten little fool, or words to that effect.

In the event, it was decided that because of the youth and inexperience of the little fool a court martial was not recommended, but that the officer was to be informed that he had incurred the grave displeasure of the Air Council. Perhaps they were kinder and more understanding than he deserved. Frighten him a bit and maybe, as Kipling nearly said, he will learn about women—and men—from that.

There was very good shooting. Sand grouse, snipe, duck of many species, teal, mallard, pintail, even geese if you were lucky, black partridge and chukor. Most of the shooting entailed an expedition of several days and called for a motor vehicle of some sort. Usually ex-WD Model T Fords. I was lucky; I bought a very nice DISS Delage tourer from a New Zealander. He had had it fitted out for long-range desert journeys, with two forty-gallon petrol tanks, one on each running board, a forty-gallon water tank and three spare wheels.

The marshes at Baquba, up the Diala river, were our favourite ground. The Delage could carry three, plus two Ascaris (native soldiers), who acted as beaters, personal bodyguards and servants.

I got to know several of the Shaikhs, so generally we received the greatest possible Bedouin hospitality, but were always equipped to fend for ourselves.

The Baquba marshes were alive with duck, as I know to my cost. Leading a flight of three aircraft very early one morning from Hinaidi to Khanakin, I chose just for the hell of it to fly the entire route at nought feet. We roared across the marshes at 5 am. The duck rose in clouds in front, behind, on both sides, on and on. Before we could climb away we had collided with hundreds of them. There were feathers everywhere and the interplane struts and flying wires were festooned with entrails. It is a miracle we were not all three wrecked. Inspecting the aircraft on landing, we had suffered almost as much damage as if we had been through flak. There were duck, cooked to a turn, wedged between the cylinders of the Jupiters, there were gaping holes in the leading edges of all the wings and the birds that had crashed through were lying hard against the main spars; one windscreen was shattered and all three propellers damaged. We flew back to base in that condition; there was no choice. No court of enquiry, no court martial, no reprimand, no repercussions, just one more bit of fun and games.

Large birds have always been a hazard to flying; I collided with a kite hawk at 6,000 feet in the Kurdish hills which knocked out the port rear outer interplane strut, reducing aileron control to nearly nothing, and necessitated us flying for the next hour with the stick hard over to starboard and lots of rudder to correct the yaw, but we got down in one piece. Less lucky was a pilot on the North West Frontier in India who hit a rock eagle. He spun in and was killed.

Birds are sometimes seen at very high altitude. Once in Australia, cruising along somewhere between Sydney and Wagga at 14,000 feet, I saw and flew alongside, for long enough to identify it, an ibis.

The first flight over Everest, by the expedition led by Flight Lieutenant the Marquis of Clydesdale in 1930, encountered a skein of geese at 21,000 feet.

Usually at Baquba we did the morning and evening duck flight and walked the dry ground and cultivations during the day for chukor and black partridge. Sometimes the Shaikh would have a big shooting party, which always included some Baghdad Arabs in European dress. On these days the duck would be driven by an army of excited and noisy tribesmen and chicos (boys) and the whole thing was fraught with danger, though not necessarily for the duck.

The feasting afterwards was what everybody had come for, and the less time spent messing about in the mud in pointed yellow shoes the better.

I never saw geese on this ground, though they must have used the marsh. Generally, they preferred those vast sheets of brackish water which at certain times of the year covered the salt pans. These were quite devoid of cover and the geese were therefore impossible to approach. We tried stalking them with rifles, with little success, and the only way to get a shot was to drive the car to the down-wind side, let two guns out on the blind side, where they lay prone, then drive the car round to the other side, get out and walk straight in. You hoped to drive the geese over the other two, but it seldom worked.

The nearest sand grouse shooting was at Ctesiphon, near the bombing and gunnery ranges. Here two guns might expect to kill twenty or thirty brace in a couple of hours. The method is the same wherever sand grouse are shot.

You lie up at the only water hole for miles around and wait for the birds to come in for their evening drink. The first few shots will send them away, but as the need for water becomes urgent they will face any barrage and just keep on coming. It seems a bit unsporting, but there were hundreds of them and the game was a welcome change in the mess from curried water buffalo or roast goat.

The sand grouse is not a grouse at all, nor even remotely like one, except for a bit of feathering on the legs. In size and coloration it is more like a golden plover, but with a wide wingspan. The wing is long and narrow like that of a swift or a falcon, and the birds are very very fast.

I have made the shooting sound easy, but that was not so. They come in on a long slanting approach at great speed and, at the sound of the guns, they wheel and rocket upwards, in the way teal do when they are shot at.

The bags of up to forty brace were achieved only with the expenditure of three or four times that number of cartridges. The sand grouse is a very sporting bird and more difficult than most other game.

There were ibex and black bear in Kurdistan and Tigris salmon (Nile perch) in the river, but without doubt the finest wildlife territory in Iraq was the Hammar Lakes in the south east, where dwelt the marsh Arabs in a wilderness of reeds and water covering an area the size of Wales. It was from here that Gavin Maxwell obtained the otters which figured in *Ring of Bright Water*.

Iraq has always attracted archaeologists, naturalists and explorers, and one of the few interesting things about the featureless maps we used in a featureless land were the dotted red lines indicating the route taken by some explorer or other, and simply annotated 'Blunt 1878', 'Leachman 1910' or 'Holt 1920–22'. They were still at it; Philby was tramping about somewhere in the southern desert, as was that most famous and intrepid lady, Freya Stark, and of course there was Gertrude Bell, more or less retired by now and often to be seen in Baghdad knocking back double brandies in some bar or other. She could eat two pilot officers for breakfast.

Our French neighbours of the Armée de L'Air in Syria also had their sporting diversions. Predictably different from ours and with official blessing. They might have had some good fishing and shooting too, but probably could not spare the time.

CHAPTER 5

The French squadrons in Syria were based at Damascus, Aleppo and Deir es Zor. They had only recently discarded their World War I Breguet 19s and were equipped with the Potez 25. This was a sturdy but ugly great chunk of an aeroplane of sesquiplane configuration, powered by the liquid-cooled 450hp Lorraine engine of 12 cylinders arranged in three banks of four, like our Napier Lion. The Potez had a maximum speed of 129mph and cruised at 95.

The squadrons in Iraq each had their opposite number in Syria. We of 55 liaised with the Aleppo squadron. One year they would visit us for joint air exercises and the following year we would visit them for a stay of three days. The flying part was routine. The (unofficial) object of the exercise as far as the pilots were concerned was to outdo each other in a rip-roaring round of non-stop hospitality, each according to his national style.

In our case the formal guest night was sedate and well-behaved up to the loyal toast and the National Anthem, played by the squadron band and followed by the 'President' and the 'Marseillaise'. From this moment on there followed the usual wild and dangerous games, as played in any British mess or ward room anywhere in the world, during which all of the glass and most of the furniture was smashed and somebody inevitable broke, if not a leg or arm, then certainly a collar-bone or rib. But no women, strictly no women—there weren't any. Not that our French friends minded much. The whisky, to which they were hardly accustomed but insisted on having, soon destroyed such carnal desires as might have been entertained.

At Aleppo things were different. The dinner was always good and the wine more so, and as that took hold inhibitions vanished.

The French had a neat showing-off trick in which one man would hold a bottle of champagne high above his head with both hands while another slashed off the neck of the bottle with a sabre. Bottle after bottle . . . *naturellement, les Anglais* must emulate their hosts. Cohen (we called him 'Nugget' because the CO was once misguided enough to say he was worth his weight in gold), who flew as my passenger on this particular trip and who later became Chief of the New Zealand Air Staff, was the first to try it. He held the bottle, while some other ass slashed away with the sabre. His aim was poor; the blade cut the bottle clean in two half-way up, removing a large slice of Nugget's left hand in the process. The Medicine Major fixed it up and the party continued.

Then on came the nautch girls; belly dancers, real ones from the officers' brothel on the base. Could it be that we had joined the wrong Air Force? The girls danced on the dining table in among the silver and glass and you were encouraged to make your choice and, with the Commandant's gracious permission, take your temporary leave. Perhaps crouching by a water hole waiting for the sand grouse to flight in is a more rewarding occupation.

The morning of our departure was anti-climax. We were going to show 'em a real close formation take-off. None of this sloppy French-style flying, with everybody half a mile apart. Wing-tip tucked inside wing-tip—that's us, that's 55.

Unfortunately my aeroplane had recently been fitted with experimental landing gear for tropical tests, including duralumin disc wheels. A little less than half way along the take-off run, but with the tail nicely up, the starboard wheel chose that moment to disintegrate. The axle of course dug into the sand and the whole thing cartwheeled neatly over, luckily coming to rest on its nose and not on its back. At the time I hadn't the remotest idea why I I had suddenly found myself in this undignified position. The take-off was delayed long enough to make sure that Nugget and I were each in one piece, whereupon the squadron abandoned me to my fate and to the French, and p'd/o to Baghdad, with Cohen now sharing the rear cockpit with the gunner of O'Donnel's aircraft. It was three days before O'Donnel returned for me. Three days of which I remember little. The aircraft had to stay until we could fly in a fitter, a rigger and the spare parts.

The three single-engined squadrons were responsible for the inspection and maintenance of forty or so landing grounds scattered around the country and sited for strategical or tactical reasons. Some were just a bit of more or less flat ground with corner markers and a white circle in the middle. The more important ones, especially those on the line of flight to such places as Damascus which were beyond the fuel range of the aircraft, had underground petrol, oil and water storage. Such a one was LG5 at Rutbah Wells; where the hell's Rutbah Wells? Others serving a vital operational role had in addition bomb and ammunition storage.

The LG's on my flights inspection list were all in mountain territory and sometimes it became necessary to try to establish new ones. One one occasion I set out with three aircraft, a week's rations for six and three hundred rupees in a canvas bag.

The brief was to inspect, repair as necessary and renew the markers on landing grounds along the Persian border, in the area Altun Kopri–Chemchemal–Sulaimaniya–Penjwin, and to reconnoitre, select and if possible, establish a new landing ground north-east of the Little Zab River.

We made base camp on the river bank at Altun Kopri and parked the aircraft in a three-pointed star, tails outward, to give a full 360° field of fire with the Lewis guns, just in case. This obsession with a good field of fire from the rear cockpit of a grounded aircraft was not just fanciful 'bull'.

A few years earlier, in this same area—near Sulaimaniya to be precise—when 8 squadron were still in Iraq, one of their DH9As, flown by Flying Officer Vintcent, had been forced down near the target he had just been bombing. A very large crowd of infuriated Kurdish warriors rushed in on the stranded aircraft, attacking from every quarter.

Vintcent, a very big and tough man (a lesser mortal would not have had the physical strength to do it, since it usually took four airmen to lift the tail of a Ninak), hoisted the tail bodily on to his shoulder, while his passenger, Flight Lieutenant J.I.T. Jones, a 1914–18 fighter 'ace', did sterling work with the Lewis gun in the rear cockpit, warding off the vengeful tribesmen.

Vintcent walked the 9A round and round for over an hour in the baking sun, until some Sopwith Snipes of 1 squadron appeared on the scene and kept the Kurds at bay long enough for another 9A to land and rescue Jones and Vintcent.

The rations we had with us were only to be used if there was nothing else, because normally on this sort of operation we lived off the country, swapping cigarettes for scrawny chickens and undersized eggs where possible, but more often by scrounging, which I regret to say was a euphemism for stealing. This was left to the troops, who were good at it, and no questions were asked. They were quite capable of scrumping an orange grove, milking a goat or knocking off a sheep, so we never went to bed hungry.

We did the inspection and repair jobs first; this is what the rupees were for—to pay the natives for the work. Now we started on the serious business of finding a piece of comparatively level ground with good approaches. A tall order in this tall country. One valley is much like another. We flew on; nothing, no chance of a landing anywhere. Over the next ridge, and the next—and suddenly there it was. A flattish patch of green covering about fifteen acres, a village, sheep, goats, horses. My own private Shangri-La. Break up the formation, go right down for a low level look-see. No great fissures in the ground, no rocks, no boggy patches, as far as one could tell, and approaches as good as you could get in this kind of country; so fire a white light to see where the wind is. A white Very cartridge makes more smoke than a red or green one. Also scares the daylights out of the natives—quite unintentionally. Make a dummy run right down to the point of touch-down. Looks all right; full throttle, climb away and try it again. Okay, we are on the ground and the right way up. Fire a green light to bring the other two in, taxi into line and switch off. By this time the entire village had arrived. We addressed ourselves to the obvious senior citizen. Bits of Arabic, bits of Urdu, lots of troops' Hindustani; no good, back to sign language. The Headman invited us to the village. I posted one airman to maintain guard on the aircraft. No, we must all come to the village. More signs and dumb-show charade, marching up and down in front of the aircraft with a muzzle-loading flintlock borrowed from a villager. Of course! An armed man detailed to each aircraft by the patriarch. *Now* will you come to the village? It seemed churlish not to. Arrived in the village, we sat cross-legged on superb carpets laid on the bare ground and, forming a half-circle facing our hosts, we waited. We had taken off at around 7am; it was now nearly ten. Coffee, the ritual two cups each, exchange cigarettes, and wait. Small talk is difficult in sign language and it is not done to state your business until invited to do so. We knew the form; they were killing the sheep and the chickens. So we sat—four solid hours—but at last it came; food, glorious food, set down in front of each of the six guests in one of those enormous copper trays four feet in diameter, each holding half a dozen spit-roasted chickens, together with a large bowl of rice, another of fried eggs and yet another of lamb stewed with saffron and almonds. The bottoms of the trays were lined with chapaties.

We tucked in, using the right hand only of course, since the left was reserved for the nastier human functions; we knew our manners. Ever tried picking up a fried egg in the fingers? Easy when you know how. You palm a piece of chapati, invert it over an egg and, like an Aussie Jackeroo rolling a cigarette with one hand, you scoop and twirl, ending up with an egg roll, the yolk of which then trickles down your chin. Our hosts did not eat; the tribesmen and kids stood silent and goggle-eyed. We ate till it hurt; it was customary. We belched politely to indicate that we could eat no more, and at a sign from the old one the villagers fell upon the food and wolfed it all in seconds. Then came water melons, nicely chilled from the village cold store, a cave into which impacted snow, cut into blocks, is stacked every winter and which lasts right through the summer.

Now it was permissible to state our business. Payment was agreed. The work of marking the ground was completed. We exchanged gifts, said our salaams and departed. One last job: photograph the field and terrain when airborne. A great day's work; higher authority *will* be pleased. Like hell it will! A little matter of frontier violation to be laughed off—Shangri-La was twenty miles inside Persia.

I have scarcely mentioned 30 squadron based at Mosul, partly because 84 were our special friends and deadly rivals, and partly because 30's sphere of operational responsibility extended north and west to the Turkish border, as a consequence of which we saw them less often; but they too suffered under, or put up with, or tolerated (depending on the point of view) a slightly dotty commanding officer.

I cannot help feeling that at Air Ministry, in the department of the Air Member for Personnel, there was a section which had a great big file containing a list of names headed 'Squadron Leaders General Duties—bracket dotty close bracket, Iraq for the use of.' Every time there was a vacancy for a squadron commander in 30,

55 or 84, some junior staff officer, in silent protest at being at Air Ministry and working on the principle that if you have several squadrons of crackpots it's just as well to send another one out to take charge, would solemnly stick a pin in this list and the chap so selected found himself in due course aboard a troopship heading East.

Or it may have been that people generally, pilot officers no less than squadron leaders, became progressively dottier with each succeeding month in a country like Iraq.

Mosul had a slightly more equable climate than Hinaidi or Shaiba. It was closer to the hills and got some quite heavy rain at certain seasons. The aerodrome even sprouted grass once in a while. Real green grass, but it could become waterlogged and very, very soft. In such conditions an aircraft could become bogged down and immovable, or worse nose over, or even turn right over on to its back.

Taking off a fairly heavy aircraft and suddenly hitting very soft ground is analagous to belting down the runway in a more sophisticated later aeroplane, for example the nose-heavy Griffon-engined Spitfire XIV (and by heaven were they nose heavy!), and slapping the brakes hard on when the tail was nicely up.

Our dotty friend at Mosul invented an aerodrome serviceability gauge. This consisted of a six-foot pole which at its lower end was calibrated in inches, with a wooden platform at the twelve inch mark. At the top of the pole there was a hole through which an iron pin or a ten-inch nail was loosely fitted.

On the pin you rested a standard lead ballast weight. I have forgotten what they weighed, but let us say ten pounds, and of course they had a hole in the middle.

The duty pilot was instructed to walk about all over the aerodrome, place his pole on the soft patches and pull out the pin, whereupon the ballast weight would drop on to the little platform and drive the pole into the ground.

The number of inches that the pole was driven into the ground was supposed to indicate the degree of unserviceability or otherwise of the surface, but by what subtle calculations of weight, time and distance travelled the pilot was supposed to arrive at his decision, I know not.

Anyhow, on the first and need I say only time this technological marvel was used, the duty pilot reported "aerodrome serviceable, sir", and the CO, putting theory into practice, quite rightly prepared to be the first pilot to taxi out and take off.

I will not labour it. You can guess the rest. Yes, he sank in axle-deep and ended up flat on his back, to the undisguised joy of all beholders, who could have told him the airfield was unserviceable without going to all that trouble.

CHAPTER 6

How will you manage
To cross alone
The autumn mountain
Which was so hard to get across
Even when we went the two of us together?

Princess Daihaku,
Japan, seventh century

All this time, tension had been building up between the Kurds and the hated Arabs. The Air Officer Commanding, Ludlow-Hewitt, sent the following despatch to the Chief of the Air Staff in London.

D.O.9

Air Headquarters,
Iraq Command,
Hinaidi.
6th February, 1931.

Dear Air Chief Marshal,

Very many thanks for your letter of the 23rd January.

2. Shaikh Mahmud, as you anticipated, is still giving us a good deal of trouble and I am afraid that the Iraq Government are spending a lot of money on winter operations against him. The difficulty arises over the fact that the country is now administered and policed, which it was not in your day. Unfortunately, many of the police posts are miserably weak and inadequate. As Shaikh Mahmud moves about collecting his contributions of money and men, he attacks or stages attacks against these posts. In one instance where the police post was quite indefensible, the twenty police surrendered and he took their rifles and 3,000 rounds of ammunition. As, of course, the capture of any police post by Shaikh Mahmud is a severe blow to the prestige of the Iraq Government and as these posts are incapable in many cases of looking after themselves, the Iraq Government find themselves compelled to send out troops to relieve the posts. Hence, these operations. Had we no police posts we could practically disregard Shaikh Mahmud's movements. But the

withdrawal of the police would be so serious an admission of defeat and helplessness that it is not thought practicable. Ever since I have been here I have been pressing the Iraq Government to improve the defences of their posts and I think that they are beginning to realise the necessity of doing this.

3. Meanwhile we cannot do very much in the way of air action. The people themselves are not hostile. Shaikh Mahmud inflicts himself upon their villages one after another, and even where they prepared to resist him they would be helpless to do so. Information as to his whereabouts is necessarily uncertain. The Iraq Government have not carried out their obligations to the Kurds and we do not want to appear to be supporting a defective and unjust administration by bombing villagers who are quite prepared to be friendly and cannot be held responsible for the trouble. Consequently the bombing of villages is not advisable on any count. It would do Shaikh Mahmud no harm and do us no good. We must warn the villages. Shaikh Mahmud then evacuates the place and goes elsewhere and we punish villagers who are only too thankful to see Shaikh Mahmud go. There is in fact no object to be gained. I had arranged to make an exception a few days ago when it looked as if the military operations by the Iraq Army might result in trapping Shaikh Mahmud in a few inaccessible villages in the Avroman mountains. In the event of this situation arising we made full arrangements to bomb the villages in order to force Shaikh Mahmud out into the open where he could be dealt with by aircraft and troops. Here there was something to be gained by bombing a village or at least threatening to bomb it. However, as was to expected, he escaped before the net closed.

4. As you see, therefore, there is no opportunity for the application of air action in the conventional manner. There is no point in bombing helpless friendly villagers out of their villages and destroying their property while the real enemy, Shaikh Mahmud, merely moves off to pastures new. Occasionally we get a chance of shooting up parties of his men in the open by daylight, but most of their movements have been carried out at dusk or during the night. I am afraid, therefore, that there is little prospect of there being any opportunity for decisive air action in the Kurdish hills just now.

5. Our plan of operations for the spring is as follows:

(a) To satisfy the legitimate aspirations of the Kurds by urging the Iraq Government to take the necessary political action to fulfil their obligations. It is hoped in this way to prevent any extension of the trouble in Kurdistan, and leave us free to deal with Shaikh Mahmud in the Spring.
(b) To raise a mobile force of 300 police whose job it will be to keep on Shaikh Mahmud's tracks, keep him moving and harry him in every way possible.
(c) To send out Iraq Army columns, probably two, to try and restrict Shaikh Mahmud's movements and facilitate the task of the police.
(d) By the combined movement of the Iraq Army columns and the police with the help of air reconnaissance to attempt to bring Shaikh Mahmud to action or compel him to cross the frontier.

6. He is very disinclined to go back to Persia as the Persians themselves are on the war path and if they catch him he is not likely to receive much consideration at their hands.

I am not optimistic about the success of our Spring operations if they come off, but the Iraq Army will gain experience and their activity is likely to prevent serious trouble in Kurdistan. 7. Will you please let me know the dates you expect to be in Palestine, as if possible I should like to fly over to see you there if you cannot come to Baghdad. 8. The High Commissioner is doing quite a lot of flying in his Moth but for the most part only local flying. We have persuaded him to do a tour in the Kurdish districts with a view to trying to clear up the misconceptions which the Kurds seem to have about our policy in Kurdistan. We shall presumably take him round most of his tour by air but on that occasion he will travel as a passenger in a Wapiti.

Yours etc.
(Sd.) E. R. Ludlow-Hewitt

My log book records:

'March 3rd. Wapiti J9847. Self—Corporal Bailey. 3 hrs 45 mins. Recco Sulaimaniya–Surdesh road.

74

March 3rd. J9847. 3 hrs 05 mins. Recco Sulaimaniya–Muan–
Penjwin.
March 4th. J9847. 3 hrs 50 mins. Recco Qara Dagh Valley.'

There was a build-up of tribesmen. We were fired on. Shaikh
Mahmud was on the war path.

On the 8th the squadron moved to Sulaimaniya and became,
together with three battalions of Iraq infantry, a brigade of Syrian
levies, two squadrons of cavalry and two companies of armoured
cars, 'Sulforce'.

The airfield at Sulaimaniya, 3500ft above sea level, was a pocket
handkerchief perched on the side of a mountain just below the
village. You landed up the hill and took off down it, irrespective
of wind speed and direction. Not everybody made it every time.
Local Syrian levies barracks were close to and uphill from the
landing ground and their British officers' mess right on the
threshold of the field. Always, immediately after take-off we would
test and warm our guns by firing two or three long bursts. We
thought it a great joke to do this by diving at the mess and firing
over the roof—day after day, just after dawn. What tedious little
bores we must have been. Why we didn't kill somebody I cannot
imagine, nor indeed why somebody out of sheer exasperation
didn't kill some of us.

We lived under canvas and at first had a commandeered house
as mess. Later, when more stores had been flown in by 70 squadron,
we had a field mess set up in a large tent I.P. (Indian pattern).

On the 9th I see from my log book Corporal Bailey and I in
J9847 did a 3 hour 50 minute reccy of Khana Kuwa and the Qara
Dagh valley, followed by three sorties of 1 hour 50 minutes each
in our first air action, the very first time I had done the thing for
which I had been trained—fired my guns and dropped my bombs
for real. My log book merely recorded front and rear gun and
low-level bombing with 20lb Coopers, anti-personnel bombs.
9 hours 20 minutes is a lot of flying in a single-engined aeroplane
in one day.

55, like all the squadrons in Iraq except for 70, was a GP (general
purpose) squadron. We were not army co-operation and had had
no training in army co-op techniques or procedures. We had to
learn it quickly and improvise. There was no radio, neither air-to-
air nor ground-to-air, so if the ground force wished to communicate with an aircraft it used a limited range of ground strip

signals; but anything in the nature of a detailed message or request demanded the ability to pick up a message bag from the ground.

Properly equipped army co-operation squadrons had a pick-up hook below the aircraft which could be lowered, not unlike the arrester gear on a deck-landing aeroplane, and to complement this the ground forces used a device similar to rugby goal-posts but without the crossbar. The message bag, with red and yellow streamers, was attached to the lower part of a loop of cord strung across the top of the poles. You lowered your hook, dived, flattened out at the right moment and *voila* you got the message. If it called for an answer you wrote your reply, put it in the weighted bag, rolled the streamers neatly, bag outermost, flew back over the column and dropped it. Fine—except that we had no hooks and the ground forces had no nice tubular telescopic goal-posts.

From the village Suk the senior NCOs got hold of some mild steel $\frac{5}{8}$ inch rod. From this the fitters improvised some pick-up hooks, one of which by some ingenious method they hinged at one end to the axle of my aeroplane's undercarriage. To the hook end they fixed a long stout cord and ran it up through the floor of the rear cockpit, where it could be made fast to a cleat. Now to try it; no good, the hook would not stay in the lowered position because of the slipstream, so we weighted it with a standard lead ballast weight. These were round flat weights with a hole in the middle, which were carried on spigots inside the fuselage down by the stern post on occasions when an aircraft was flown without a rear seat passenger or equivalent load. It worked perfectly; the hook stayed down when released.

Now for the goal-posts. What would the army always have available? Rifles, of course. What could be simpler? Two rifles with fixed bayonets stuck in the ground say ten feet apart, with the cord strung through the butt traps. Good idea, let's try it.

A .303 rifle stuck on end is less than four feet high. I tried it once, twice, three times. "Too high," shrieked Corporal Bailey, "lower, lower, lower!" "Damn it, I'll do it this time if it kills us." Famous last words.

I stuffed the nose down once more. The ground rushed up. "Okay," yelled Corporal Bailey, "we're doing nicely." There was a rending crash as bits of two rifles flew in all directions, and an almighty bang as the port tyre burst, slashed by a bayonet. We had the message bag all right, but not on the hook. We made a cross-wind landing on the starboard wheel, did a gentle ground loop as the speed dropped off and the port wheel touched the ground, and there we were. The message cord was wrapped neatly round the propeller-boss. The idea was sound enough, even though the flying was not, but we had learned a lot and used this method throughout the campaign, mostly in atrocious territory (the army had a touching faith in the skill of pilots and the versatility of aeroplanes). There were no untoward incidents, apart from a few bullet holes, but co-operation between air and ground forces improved enormously with the appointment of an airman for liaison duties with the column. Flight Lieutenant Webster no less, who in 1927 had won the Schneider Trophy race and knew a thing or two about flying.

During the three months of operations we lost a lot of aircraft and several pilots and crew, sometimes directly or indirectly as a result of enemy fire, but more often through misjudgment in difficult terrain. One would hardly imagine that primitive tribesmen armed, apart from a few smuggled or stolen machine guns, only with rifles of uncertain ancestry and erratic performance could achieve any success against aircraft. They did have the advantage however in those awesome valleys of being able to fire from above as well as below.

This business of tribesmen shooting down aircraft with rifles must sound ludicrous and unlikely, but it must be remembered that by comparison with modern aircraft machines like DH9As, Snipes and Wapitis were not only vulnerable and slow, but were also flying just a few feet above the ground. If my veracity is in doubt, I should point out that during the Arab revolt in the southern desert, which occurred only ten years before the events I relate, no less than eleven aircraft were shot down and a further fifty-seven, though able to get back to base, were a total write-off as a result of accurate rifle fire.

Every pilot in the squadron flew at least one sortie a day, and often two or three, so the tribesmen had plenty of practice against low-flying aircraft.

For March 19th my log book records the following:
'Wapiti J9847. 2 hrs 35 mins. Bombing in Qara Dagh valley 18 × 20lb bombs 2 × 112lb bombs 750 rounds SAP. 2 hrs. Second raid in Qara Dagh 24 × 20lb bombs 2 × 112lb bombs 750 rounds

SAP. 1 hr 45 mins. Third raid in the Qara Dagh 24 × 20lb bombs 2 × 112lb bombs 500 rounds SAP.'

At the end of the day J9847 had 75 bullet holes in her, including one straight up into the pilot's seat which, fortunately for all concerned, only penetrated half-way through the folds of silk of the parachute pack. The mountain men were no novices when it came to a bit of shooting.

The rudder, fin and tailplane were in shreds and 9847 had to go back to Hinaidi for a refit. New engine, new tailplane and wings and fuselage recovered.

A pilot had his own machine and his own fitter and rigger. You had your aeroplane rigged to your liking, so that it responded to your own particular touch and style of flying. If for some reason someone else had been flying your aircraft you knew it the moment you got it off the ground, or even before, and cursed the unknown or known culprit for a ham-handed SOB. Equally, if you flew someone else's aeroplane you thought, and seldom hesitated to say, how could anyone possibly put up with such a God-awful crate?

So I flew 9635, but it was just an aeroplane; it had neither character nor personality, though the pilot who regularly flew it probably loved it.

The depot did a good job on 9847, demonstrating both alacrity and skill. She went on March 27th and was back in my hands on April 27th. We lost no time getting into business. On the day she came back my log book records:

'J9847 2 hrs 95 mins. Raid on Sarakan.'

On the 28th we flew two sorties and on the 29th three, attacking targets at Gola, Norik and Chemak.

Chaps got killed; aeroplanes were destroyed. Sergeant Pilot Anthony flew into some trees with a full load of bombs and blew himself up. Jimmy Wells was shot down in hostile territory, breaking only his collar-bone and arm, but becoming a captive of the tribesmen. We got him back when hostilities ended, with the aid of 'the chit'. It did work sometimes; but unfortunately for Wells he was a prisoner for nearly two months, without of course receiving any medical attention.

The Kurds treated him quite well, in their fashion, and did the best they could for him in accordance with tribal surgical practice, which was to kill a goat, skin it and wrap the uncured skin around Wells' shoulder and arm in the form of a nicely hairy and smelly sling. The theory behind this piece of witch doctoring is that as the skin dries out and shrinks it pulls the broken bones together. In practice it works well, but since the fracture was not properly set, by the time the prisoner was released his arm and shoulder had mended all awry.

He was flown immediately to the RAF hospital at Hinaidi, where his arm and collar-bone were rebroken and reset, but he was never fit to fly again.

I met him once during the war when he was doing an administrative job somewhere and noticed that he had a withered and almost useless right arm.

I had my altercation with the kite hawk flying over the Qara Dagh (Black Mountain). Gardiner, our incorrigible CO, said we didn't come low enough on our dive-bombing runs, so showed us how and put the fragments from his fragmentation bombs through his own main-planes. The thing was like a colander and though flyable, just, it was officially a write-off.

Pussy Foster, flying in supplies in a Vickers Victoria, crashed on landing and smashed all the gramophone records we had asked for, and we cursed him for a clumsy ox.

Staff officers from Air Headquarters, Hinaidi, came up to find out if we knew what we were supposed to be doing. They usually stayed about a week. The squadron cynics reckoned they only came for long enough to qualify for a campaign medal before beating it back to their desks, but there was in fact some doubt about whether a certain tribe and village had sided with Mahmoud or were still loyal to Baghdad.

Gardiner thought there was only one way to find out. "Go thou, Carr," he said—in this Old Testament country people were inclined to wax biblically lyrical, rubbing shoulders as we frequently did with Nineveh, Ur of the Chaldees, Babylon and Hitt, even the Garden of Eden, which according to learned savants and theologians was in southern Iraq, not far from Shaiba. It must have altered a very great deal since Adam's time—"Go thou in steam chicken Mark IIA J9847, thine own Wapiti. Descend upon Shah Nadri and discover unto me whether he that dwelleth within the gate be mine enemy or no."

Now if you paused to analyse such an order, you might conclude:

(a) that an aeroplane on the ground is bereft of all but the barest tactical capability and that a pilot similarly placed is not a fat lot of use either,

(b) that if the natives *were* hostile the likelihood of your safe return to base to report the fact might be minimal, and

(c) that the person giving the order must be slightly round the bend.

But you didn't analyse an order. You didn't even think it odd. Nor did you say, "Why can't Joe do it?" In fact, if someone had asked you how you would find out, you would have said "By going there, of course." So you saluted smartly, fell out and went to find Corporal Bailey, for heaven's sake, which would not be difficult. He would be with the aircraft, fussing over his beloved engine, supervising the refuelling, checking the ammunition for both guns and keeping an eagle eye on the armourers to make sure that they set the fuses and nose pistols correctly on the bombs.

If it had gone wrong, good old George Cecil Gardiner would have been very cross and would without doubt have taken the entire squadron in once, twice or as many times as it took to obliterate the village. Great stuff, and probably good for a DSO, but not much consolation for poor Carr and Bailey.

So there we were, circling around low down over Shah Nadri, partly to see if anyone was tempted to fire a round or two, and partly to pick out a place on which to land, which we eventually did.

I taxied broadside on to the village, to give Bailey a good arc of fire with the Lewis gun between main-plane and tail to cover me, left the engine ticking over for the quick getaway (I hope) and walked towards the village.

I had my .455, but kept it in its holster; it would not do to appear ill-intentioned. What the Kurds thought of this silly little Ferangi with the pink face it was impossible to guess.

A dozen tribesmen, armed to the teeth as always, advanced to meet me. We stopped and exchanged the formal greeting demanded by custom and protocol (please God, don't let me forget the words): "*Salaam aleikum*—Peace be unto you." "*Wa aleikum es salaam*—And on you peace." On my head and my heart (touching forehead and chest with the finger-tips of the right hand): "*El hamdu lillah*—Praise God." "*In sha allah*—If God will."

We exchanged the inevitable cigarettes. Bowing gravely in farewell, I turned and walked to the aircraft as casually as I knew how, trying desperately not to run and wondering what it would feel like to be shot in the back. I climbed in, waved goodbye and slammed the throttle through the gate. To hell with the Sutton harness, let's get out of here fast.

I was able to report "village friendly, sir."

A few days later they joined Shaikh Mahmud. They had no choice; fifty or so of his fighting men had marched in on a press-gang expedition. Mahmud surrendered in May, but not before I had the good fortune to witness from the air what must have been one of the last cavalry charges by any army.

On April 5th we were again in action in the Qara Dagh at Awa Barika, where the troops, after a forced march of thirty miles, were facing Mahmud's main force. As we flew over the column on our third sortie that day, sure enough there was the inevitable ground strip signal, requesting a message pick-up. Oh God, not again, not down there; a steep-sided canyon, with a rock-strewn floor, damn all room to turn and too much turbulence, is no place to be frigging about low down with a full load of bombs, as poor old Sergeant Anthony discovered, but too late to do him any good.

Blast the bloody army, you'd think they would have more sense! let's pretend we haven't seen it. "Hook down, Corporal Bailey." "Hook down, sir." The message read "Held up by heavy and concentrated fire from the fort at the head of the valley. Please destroy." "Please destroy"; who the hell do they think they are?

I wrote in reply, "Happy to oblige", came back over the column, dropped the message, then took a look at the target.

At the top end of the Qara Dagh valley one side of the mountain face had great gaps every half mile or so, making it look for all the world like some gigantic row of dragon's teeth. Through these fissures the wind would roar and, hitting the rock face on the other side, create a series of fearsome vortices, in which the aeroplane was tossed about like a shuttlecock.

"Come on then, Corporal Bailey, what are we hanging about for?"

"*I'm* not hanging about, sir, I'm just standing here in this lousy bloody cockpit waiting for my pilot to make his mind up."

"Very well, if you have primed Mr. Lewis's patent musket and fitted a new flint, we might as well get started."

We made two or three passes with front and rear guns to get the feel of it, to judge the right moment to pull out and climb, and to see how much room we had, if any, in which to turn. Then two sighting runs with salvos of Coopers, six at a time off the inner racks, and on the next run the remaining twelve Coopers. For this rather hit or miss low-level bombing there were no sighting aids. You relied on judgement of speed, angle of descent and drift. It was rather like trying to spear fish in a barrel.

I used to try to maintain a steady angle of descent of about 30° and release my bombs just as the target passed beneath the leading edge of the lower main-planes. Okay, this time; the 112s, both of 'em. Lovely. Slap through the front door.

The Coopers were always fused instantaneous, that is to say to explode on contact, but the 112s on low-level dive bombing had a two-second delayed action fuse to enable you to get clear before they burst and to obtain good penetration.

We climbed away and came back over for another pass with front and rear guns, but there was no need. Half the fort had gone. It was only built of Muttie anyway.

There was little more we could do except stooge around and watch, which is how we came to see the cavalry charge.

One sees endless cavalry charges on the cinema screen—the Charge of the Light Brigade, the US cavalry at Little Big Horn—but this was like none of those. In the films each rank of troopers is strung out in extended order in a nice straight line, as on parade. They walk, then trot, then canter and finally break into a hell-for-leather gallop. No doubt this is the correct and classic way to do it.

Our little lot down in the Qara Dagh valley either hadn't been trained in the classic tradition or didn't care. The charge was wedge-shaped, like an RAF Vee formation, and it galloped flat out from the start, straight up the valley. We cheered like mad and dived ahead of them with guns blazing. As things turned out that was a silly thing to do.

It was almost dark and time to head back to Sul. Then it happened; the engine coughed, picked up, misfired again. Petrol? Couldn't be. We had not been airborne much more than two hours. But it was. There must be a hole in the main tank. Some lousy tribesman with more luck than judgement had scored a bull. The squadron song didn't seem quite so funny now.

Change over to reserve, which will give about forty minutes flying—if it hasn't got a hole in it too. Not enough to get to Sul, but perhaps enough to get clear of the worst of the mountains and into the foothills to the west.

It would be dark, with no moon, and you know what I think about wing-tip flares. At Sul they would put out a flare path, but we couldn't get to Sul. If we were going to crash land in the dark it was better to do it where the ground didn't stand up edgeways.

So that's what we did and we were lucky. We didn't even bend the Wapiti.

Oddly enough, not for one moment did it occur to Bailey or to me to bail out. We all had this sort of pride about staying with the aeroplane come what may.

Yet it was not all bravado; most of the squadron's flying was over the desert, where it was nearly always possible to find a piece of ground suitable for a safe landing, and furthermore the search aircraft were much more likely to spot an aeroplane than two men in that immense landscape. Moreover, the machine provided shade from a pitiless sun, and held a supply of food and water sufficient to sustain life for about eight days, as well as a Very pistol and cartridges with which to fire a distress signal. In the direst extremity there was also the Lewis gun and 750 rounds.

The same considerations applied in the mountains, with one exception—finding a piece of ground.

So, unless the wings fell off or something equally embarrassing, with mere engine failure you stayed with the aircraft, mountains or no mountains. Not that engine failure, unless caused by enemy action, was all that frequent with the Bristol Jupiter. It was a fine engine and, without being conscious of it, you knew it down to the last nut, bolt and split pin. You knew it, felt it, and listened to it, from the great 14-foot propellor, through the reduction gear, to the crankshaft. You knew the nine pistons thumping up and down, the eighteen push-rods and thirty-six valves, each with two coil springs, the two magnetos giving life to eighteen spark plugs. The failure of any one of these numerous clanking bits of metal could spell disaster in these mountains, so you nursed your engine like a baby, never, except in dire need, putting the throttle through the gate, so that when the emergency arose you could demand maximum power and be pretty sure of getting it.

Corporal Bailey knew these things too and listened with an even more sensitive ear for the changing note or the misfire, for was he not engine fitter as well as gunner? It was his engine; he serviced the thing, and his life as well as the pilot's depended on his skill, knowledge and painstaking attention to detail.

You were always aware of the aeroplane itself: the four main-planes, each with its front and rear spar, how the spars were bolted on to the fuselage, the interplane struts and cross bracing wires, which held the whole contraption together and sang their little humming song to you, telling you almost as much about speed or the lack of it as did the ASI. You seldom, if ever, thought about all this; it was just that your hands and feet conveyed it all to the brain so that, if the engine missed a beat, your heart did the same.

Yet the flight instruments, rudimentary though they might be, were on occasion a surer guide to what was happening than one's backside. During an introductory flight in the high country I was formating on the flight commander during a trip to Sulaimaniya from Kirkuk. Our course took us over the northern end of the Qara Dagh, the tops of which were obscured by cloud extending up to about 15,000 feet. This meant trying to go underneath it, through the Takya Ahmad pass, a narrow gorge with near-vertical walls reaching upwards into the overcast.

It was all right to begin with, but as the floor of the valley rose so the cloud it seemed came lower, and very soon my guiding star disappeared into the murk and I lost him. No matter, watch the big P4 compass and the airspeed, grit your teeth and press on. Soon perseverance was rewarded; we shot out of the cloud into sunshine and fifty miles' visibility, and all was well—or *was* it? Where were the snow-capped mountains that should have stretched, range on range, ahead? This was foothill country and the wrong colour, and moreover the sun was inexplicably to port instead of starboard.

Without being in the least bit aware of it, I had done a complete 180° turn and straightened up on a reciprocal heading; and, because it must have been the will of Allah, I had not smeared the aeroplane and ourselves along the wall of the gorge. All of which was just fine, except for the fact that now, with ego deflated, confidence shattered and no hoary old flight commander to latch on to, I had to turn round and fly through the cloud and the bloody pass all over again. No sympathy from Hunker when we finally made it to Sul, but a piece of succinct advice, "If you can't fly in cloud, you'd better damn well learn to fly tighter formation."

Anyway, Bailey and I and the Wapiti were safely on the ground, but God alone knew where. Nor whether we were in hostile territory or not. It was no good leaving the aircraft, because we might never find our way back to it; as in the desert, an air search might locate the aeroplane within a day or two, but would seldom find the crew if they wandered off. We knew what to do. The standard drill: break out the emergency rations but eat them cold straight out of the cans—can't light a fire in case it attracts unwelcome visitors—smoke a cigarette or two, cupped in the hand to hide the glowing tip, then get some sleep. Not both at the same time, because of keeping watch, and not on the ground because of scorpions. One at a time in the front cockpit. Two hours on, two hours off. We were young and fit and could sleep standing up if we had to, but in the event we didn't have to.

There were voices, then a flickering lantern in the darkness. Not enemies, they wouldn't have made a sound, much less shown a light; they would have stalked us *ventre à terre* with infinite stealth and patience, and it is unlikely that we would have even sensed their presence until the arm across the throat and the knife in the guts. So we shouted and hallooed and were answered.

We had landed near an Iraqi police post not far from the village of Sulaiman Beg. The men had heard the aircraft and had gone in search of it, so now we had a decent meal, shared a bottle of arak with the police and got a good night's kip after all, on a couple of spare charpoys.

If this sounds like a pretty good line-shoot (which it does), I should like to disclaim any pretence of being a brilliant pilot.

Two months after this incident Professor Livingstone, the eminent eye specialist, came out to Iraq at the invitation of Air Ministry to test pilots' eyes in order to find out if two or three years exposure to desert glare had an adverse effect on visual acuity.

When Livingstone had finished with me he said, "Are you the pilot who forced landed in the dark up in Kurdistan recently?"

"Yes," I replied. "Why do you ask?"

"Well, I thought it must be you because you have quite exceptional night vision."

So the truth of the matter is that Corporal Bailey and I owe our survival to the fact that the good Lord saw fit to kit me out with a pair of cat's eyes.

That day's work at Awa Barika finally broke Mahmud's spirit, and although he slipped through the net that night while Bailey and I were snoring fit to bust at Sulaiman Beg, he surrendered a months later at Penjwin, a village within stone-throwing distance of the Persian frontier.

None of us really enjoyed fighting the Kurds, or more precisely we enjoyed the fight but wished it had not been the Kurds. Though an Islamic race, they were non-Arab and had a closer affinity with Persia than Iraq. Like all hill men they were and are a proud, stiff-necked lot and the sympathies of most people in the squadron were with the Kurds rather than the Iraqi Arabs. But their land was part of the mandated territories, and when after the 1914–18 war someone somewhere had drawn a line on a map, the Kurds found themselves, for reasons which they failed to understand, under the overlordship of the hated Arabs. However, as the squadron had a job to do, the pilots, if they had opinions, kept them to themselves.

In the forty or more years which have elapsed since we fought Mahmud, nothing has changed. Mahmud has long since gone to his Muslim paradise, where he is no doubt surrounded by beautiful dancing girls, but Mullah Mustapha Barzani, south of whose pass we preferred not to forced land or crash, donned Mahmud's mantle and even as I write is now rallying the tribesmen yet again to fight for independence.

Of course the affair has all the trendy trappings of the seventies. Barzani calls his movement the Kurdistan Democratic Party. There was nothing democratic about Mahmud, and I take leave to doubt if Barzani either is overburdened with sentiments of democracy, at least as the West understands the term. The tribesmen who will do the fighting are now (surprise, surprise!) described as 'guerrillas'.

As is only to be expected in the mid-seventies, oil too plays a role. Kirkuk is a Kurdish town. It is also the centre of Iraq's largest oilfield. So Barzani, objecting to the 'Arabisation' of Kirkuk, wants what he considers to be his share of the rich pickings.

He is said to have artillery, anti-tank and anti-aircraft weaponry, which must make a nice change from rifles, but the Iraqis are reported to be contemplating the use of poison gas. They also of course have an air force, which the Kurds do not.

The thing which has not changed is the terrain; the mountains still stand where they did. My money, if I was a betting man, would be on the Kurds, by which I do not mean to suggest that they will win the current contest any more than they won any of the previous ones.

What will happen is that the insurrection will be put down, the Kurds will as always take to the hills, and will gradually trickle back to the villages during the period of uneasy peace preceding the next conflict. Barzani is now seventy-six, but there will always be some other shaikh or mullah able, willing and ready to take over where he leaves off.

CHAPTER 7

O sons of men,
Why do you put your hands before your eyes
And play in this road as if for ever,
Which is a short passage to another place?
Where are the Kings
Whose loins jetted empires,
Where are the very strong men,
Masters of Irak?
Where are the Lords of Ispahan,
O sons of men?

Inscriptions from the City of Brass,
Arabia, twelfth century

As with soldiers on the ground, pilots and aircrew fighting a battle see the thing only as it affects them. They confine themselves to doing what they are expected to do without too much introspection and hope to stay alive, even if they pretend not to care one way or the other.

The account of the operations against Mahmud is as I saw them, and is in contrast, but not in conflict, with the wide-angle picture which Ludlow-Hewitt saw, and described in his despatch to Air Ministry and his report to Pirie at the Staff College. This despatch is in the form of a staff paper from A.1.5, which was the Air Intelligence staff of Air Headquarters Iraq Command.

The original is now in the Public Records Office, together with all the other official documents which I have reproduced.

Operations against Sheikh Mahmoud

The General Situation
The operations against Sheikh Mahmoud which took place during the months of January to the end of April 1931 consisted of two phases:
(1) Operations conducted for the relief of isolated police posts in the difficult hill country to the east of Sulaimani which were attacked or threatened by Sheikh Mahmoud and his followers.
(11) Operations in the comparatively open country of the Kifri

vicinity which were calculated to bring the rebels to action and secure the defeat and capture of Sheikh Mahmoud.

The first phase
The first phase took place in the winter months from January to mid-March when movement is greatly restricted owing to severe climatic conditions. The rebels attacked or threatened isolated detachments of police and although Iraq Army troops were sent out to relieve the threatened garrisons, movements which provoked a certain amount of guerrilla warfare, there was no opportunity of bringing the rebel forces to an engagement. Aircraft however acting in cooperation with the Iraq Army were able to inflict casualties on several occasions.

As the season advanced Sheikh Mahmoud and his followers extended their operations into the Qara Dagh, lying to the south-west of Sulaimani, a difficult and broken region suited to such an activity as the rebel forces were carrying on. The Sheikh by means of extensive propaganda was able to rally important tribal elements to his cause and further revolt broke out in the Shaikhan district on the Persian frontier between Halabja and Khaniqin. During this period—early March—the rebel forces while crossing open country between the mountain ranges were encountered by aircraft on two occasions and casualties were inflicted.

By the middle of March however the situation in the Sulaimani area was serious and Sheikh Mahmoud was in almost undisputed possession of the country from the Persian frontier as far as the Qara Dagh area south and west of Sulaimani while neighbouring tribes of the adjacent Kirkuk Liwa showed inclinations to join him.

The second phase
The centre of the revolt was now in Qara Dagh where Sheikh Mahmoud with some 400–500 followers was located. A less important outbreak had taken place in the Shaikhan area where police detachments were blockaded.

To deal with this situation it was decided to effect a concentration at Sulaimani but since the concentration could not be completed until late in March, a force was sent into the Qara Dagh on the 14th March in order to counter the rebel activity. To cooperate with these forces two flights of aircraft and 1 section of armoured cars were moved to Sulaimani.

Air operation in Shaikhan
In the meantime parties of rebels from Sheikh Mahmoud's forces had arrived in the Shaikhan area, and having invested the police engaged in illegal tax collections. The Iraq Government requested that air action should be taken to restore the situation and two flights of aircraft were moved to Khaniqin. Communication was established with the police by means of dropping and picking up messages and rebel locations were identified. Warning messages on rebel occupied localities were dropped and the villages were later bombed to destruction. The police were able to emerge from their post and in response to orders, the leading head man of the area reported to Government and made submission.

Combined operations against Sheikh Mahmoud
The main operations against Sheikh Mahmoud began on the 28th March. The general idea was to use infantry to block the passes from the area in which the rebels were located and then by means of mobile columns to so drive them as to oblige them to fight.

Sheikh Mahmoud was located at Dukan at the southern end of the Qara Dagh. Infantry posts had been established to close the main passes and cavalry swept the valley between the parallel ranges. No rebels were encountered as the Sheikh had slipped across the hills the night before the passes were closed. Air reconnaissance however discovered parties of rebels lurking in villages at the foot of the passes and these were machine gunned and bombed.

The rebels had now moved south west into the Kifri area among the nomad Jaf tribe which Sheikh Mahmoud hoped to raise (as he had done in former revolt) against the Government. The rebels were now out of convenient range of aircraft from Sulaimani and a flight was moved to a locality where it could operate more effectively.

Mobile forces of cavalry and mounted police followed up the rebels who were reported on the 4th April near Kani Qadir Miran Beg. On the 5th aircraft located them at Awa Barika and an aeroplane remained over the village throughout the day to pin the enemy to their ground and at the same time they were attacked by aircraft in relays.

The mobile forces meantime had moved at dawn and after a

forced march of 32 miles arrived at Awa Barika in the late afternoon. The rebels were immediately attacked but having prepared the village for defence could not be dislodged. The troops had to withdraw to a distance and during the night Sheikh Mahmoud and his adherents were able to slip away. They had some 40 casualties and in their departure left behind eight dead with rifles and ammunition.

The rebel leader was now in flight and having eluded the infantry posts on the Qara Dagh range and the armoured cars on the Sulaimani–Halabja road took refuge in the rugged 'massif' east of Sulaimani. After an interval for the reorganisation of forces pursuit was taken up and the Sheikh finally crossed the Persian frontier on the 23rd April being harried by aircraft while on his way.

Submission of Sheikh Mahmoud
As soon as Sheikh Mahmoud crossed the Persian frontier steps were taken to arrange cooperation with the Persian military authorities against him. Sheikh Mahmoud had however begun to realise that his revolt had failed and he asked for an interview with a representative of the High Commissioner. On the 2nd May he was presented with an ultimatum and on the 11th he came to Panjvin to meet the Government representatives and discuss terms. On the 13th he surrendered at Panjvin, was taken to Sulaimani on the 14th and on the 15th was flown to Ur on the Euphrates.

It is interesting to note that at the first meeting at Panjvin Sheikh Mahmoud went up to a Royal Air Force officer and pointing to the wings on his tunic said, "You are the people who have broken my spirit." He appeared to realise the consequences of being pinned and attacked from the air while a column approached to attack him on the ground.

A.I.5
10*th July*, 1931.

What Mahmud also said when he pointed to the wings on the pilot's tunic was, "I taught you to bomb!" I was there when he said it.

The following letter from Ludlow-Hewitt to Pirie was prompted by the fact that Pirie, who was (I think) director of studies at the staff college, had over-emphasised the role of the air force and diminished that of the army; because the operations in Kurdistan were to be used by the staff college in lectures and exercises as a classic example of 'Air Control', it was essential to get it right.

Ludlow-Hewitt was a stickler for co-operation between the services and was ahead of his time.

Air Headquarters,
'Iraq Command,
Hinaidi.
6th July, 1931.

Dear Pirie,

I have got your letter asking about Shaikh Mahmud. Your version is fairly accurate, but the following may be of some use to you to supplement your own notes.

2. When Shaikh Mahmud came over into 'Iraq from Persia he came practically alone and professing friendly, harmless intentions. He was told to clear out and stay out according to the promises he had given when he was allowed to go and live in Persia in June 1927. While continuing to protest his innocence he remained in 'Iraq. Of course, it was the obvious duty of the 'Iraqi Police to go and arrest him, but I am afraid the 'Iraqi Police unless led by British officers are not very enterprising and they did not even make the attempt. It was obviously out of the question to bomb a village just because Shaikh Mahmud was in it, especially since he gave out that he was visiting sick relatives and generally peacefully employed. Nor in fact, as you suggest, was it by any means certain where he was all the time.

3. As he consistently disobeyed all instructions to clear out, it was decided that the operations should be carried out by the 'Iraq Army, as although it was really a police job the police were not available in sufficient numbers, and therefore ground troops had to be employed.

4. The principal factors which influenced us in deciding that the 'Iraqi Army should do the job were these.

First of all we were impressed by the fact that 'Iraq would so soon have to stand on her own feet without British assistance. Her new army had never been tried under its own officers, nor had the 'Iraqi Government ever carried out any military operations under their own authority and command. It was essential that they should be given the earliest opportunity to run their own military show with as little assistance from Imperial forces as possible.

Secondly the rebel movement was a small one, well within the powers of a few battalions of the 'Iraqi Army to deal with.

Thirdly, Shaikh Mahmud's return had been brought about mainly through the action of the 'Iraqi Government themselves and their stupid ways of dealing with the Kurdish situation. Consequently we thought that the 'Iraqi Government should stand the racket of their own actions.

Fourthly, we British, although we felt that Shaikh Mahmud was to some extent a British responsibility, did not feel at all inclined to bomb innocent Kurdish villages simply because this wretched bandit chose to billet himself on them.

These two latter considerations influenced our policy throughout the operations. We felt that it was practically impossible for the Kurdish villagers to prevent Shaikh Mahmud taking up his quarters in their village and that *so long as the 'Iraqi Government were not carrying out the various concessions which they had promised to the Kurds we would not use the Air Force or Imperial troops to bolster up their maladministration.*

5. Everything pointed therefore to the need to give the 'Iraqi Army this opportunity of showing its mettle, of taking advantage of the admirable training which the operations would afford, of learning the country, of practising hill warfare and of operating under their own commanders. Hence for all these reasons it was overwhelmingly apparent that the operations should be left in the hands of the 'Iraqi Army. At the same time I undertook to provide aircraft for security and information purposes only; that is to say we felt that it would not be right for us to refuse to help the 'Iraqi Army if it got into difficulties or to refuse to provide it with reconnaissances when it was moving through extremely difficult country haunted by Shaikh Mahmud and his followers. But we would only take air action when the enemy were actually engaged with the 'Iraqi Army. Under such circumstances there would be little fear of bombing people who were not actually followers of Shaikh Mahmud. We particularly wanted to avoid attacking innocent villagers. Opportunities of attacking the enemy in the open were, of course, very rare, and only occurred on very few occasions, but we did succeed in rendering very real

help to the 'Iraqi Army in this way when they were held up by the rebels.

6. Although Shaikh Mahmud on his side scored no successes against the 'Iraqi Army, the 'Iraqi Army also scored no important successes against Shaikh Mahmud, and as the months passed, while the 'Iraqi Army got all the military training it wanted it did not succeed in making any headway against Shaikh Mahmud's movements. On the other hand time was all in favour of Shaikh Mahmud, as he moved from village to village collecting money and men. So long as he remained in the hills behind Sulaimani we felt that he could do no really great harm. But presently he moved South and West, firstly to the Halebja plain, where the 'Iraqi Army made an abortive attempt to round him up, and later into the Qara Dagh. This was beginning to get more serious and I agreed to extend air action to the extent of bombing any parties of armed Kurds found in the open in the neighbourhood in which Shaikh Mahmud's men were reported, whether they were in contact with the 'Iraqi troops or not. This resulted in one or two attacks but nothing decisive. Shaikh Mahmud and his men knew that our policy was not to bomb villages and as soon as aircraft were seen or heard they took refuge in the villages where they remained until the aircraft left. Even so we still felt that we were not justified in bombing villages upon which Shaikh Mahmud and his followers forced themselves. It is true that for the most part the villagers willingly sheltered the rebels but they had justifiable grievances against the 'Iraqi Government and also they were really not in a position to resist him.

7. Then the situation took a different turn. You no doubt remember the Jaf who graze their cattle during the winter in the foot hills south-west of the Qara Dagh. These people are always ready for a scrap and Shaikh Mahmud's continued activities soon reacted upon them. Hence on Shaikh Mahmud's arrival in the Qara Dagh we suddenly found ourselves faced by a rapid spread of the rebel movement. It was no longer simply a question of chasing an isolated bandit and his followers. We had now to deal with a rebellious movement amongst the tribes themselves. That was an entirely different situation. The Jaf had no particular grievance, neither had the inhabitants of Shaikhwan district east of the Sirwan river. These latter people had

94

welcomed parties of the rebels and started collecting Koda tax and attacking police posts.

8. I felt that now there was no question of attacking friendly villages. These tribes had clearly thrown in their lot with the rebels. Hence I now agreed to support the 'Iraqi Army by attacking rebel villages or villages sheltering rebels in the rebellious area. The result was the destruction of three villages in the Shaikhwan area after the usual warnings, and subsequently the combined attack by air and ground forces on Awa Barika, a Jaf village where we had located Shaikh Mahmud and his main force. This latter was a very interesting little operation. Shaikh Mahmud had moved down in support of the Jaf and air reconnaissance reported him in Awa Barika. The 'Iraqi Army had at last succeeded in forming a sufficiently mobile column to take advantage of such reports. At the time this report was received this mobile column was about thirty miles from the village of Awa Barika. They made a splendid forced march and reached Awa Barika that evening, finding the rebels still there. They were still there because the Air Force had been sitting over the village all day and so prevented the rebels from breaking cover and getting away. The rebels had been kept under fire from the air all day, and in the evening the mobile column arrived and made an excellent effort to rush the village, in which, however, they did not succeed in securing more than a footing. They then attempted to surround the village but darkness intervened and for some reason they did not complete their encircling movement. The rebels put up a good resistance and darkness prevented the 'Iraqi Army from exploiting their advantage. The rebels succeeded in slipping away during the night. It was a good show and was within an ace of being sensationally successful. I really think that if the mobile column had arrived an hour earlier we would have bagged the whole boiling. As it was, although Shaikh Mahmud got away he and his men suffered so severely from air bombardment that the heart was quite knocked out of them. The combination of air and ground forces used in this way was too much for them. Once located from the air he could be held there by air attack until the column came up to capture him. Thenceforward he no longer allowed the 'Iraqi Army to get within two days march of him. He made straight for the Persian frontier

and never attempted to put up any further resistance. We followed up our advantage from the air and bombed him wherever he was located until he reached and crossed the frontier.

9. The 'Iraqi Army had done very well and in particular had shown themselves excellent marchers, and when commanded by British officers they had plenty of drive. But the operations also proved that when led by their own officers the best opportunities were missed through lack of energy, initiative and drive. Another serious weakness in the 'Iraqi military organisation was the strong element of treachery which underlay and baulked the plans of the 'Iraqi commanders. I do not want to go into this here, but it is sufficient to explain that after the battle of Awa Barika Shaikh Mahmud was in an extremely difficult position. The passes over the Qara Dagh were all supposed to be held as also were the fords over the Diala. Our armoured cars closed the exits to the north-west and it should have been possible to drive him up against the Qara Dagh mountains and trap him there. However, through deliberate treachery one of the passes was left open and a bonfire was lit on top of it as a signal to him that he could pass through, which he accordingly did and escaped into the hills behind Sulaimani.

10. I have given the reasons why we did not use the Air Force decisively in the beginning. It was only when the problem ceased to be one of chasing a bandit in friendly country (strictly a police role) and became one of suppressing a rebellion of tribesmen who had no legitimate grievance against the Government that we intervened in full force. The result of our intervention was that the rebellious movement immediately broke down. The trouble in the Shaikhwan area in which there were no 'Iraqi troops was completely liquidated as a result of the destruction of the villages. In the Jaf area after the combat at Awa Barika no further trouble occurred and the Shaikhs have since submitted.

11. Shaikh Mahmud after surrendering pointed to the wings on an Air Force officer's coat and said, "You are the people who have destroyed me." He further illustrated the helplessness of the rebels against air attack when he related a story of how the rebels had come to him as the great religious leader and asked him to request Allah to prevent the aircraft from bombing them.

Left: Desert police at Rutbah Fort.

Below: No. 1 armoured car company, RAF.

Top: Shaikh Mahmud with some of his men. Mullah Mustapha Barzani is
second from left, standing.

Above: Will you have the other half, old boy?

Right: Persian Fakir, predating the hippy by 40 years—or 400 years, or
4000 years.

Top: The villagers were friendly!

Top Left: The waters of Babylon. Nobody sat down and wept.

Left: The author in J9847 at 10,000ft over the Qara Dagh country. If the engine missed a beat your heart did the same.

We three, we happy three.

Top Left: The Author.

Left: Corporal Bailey.

Right: J9847 with the disc wheels which disintegrated at Aleppo.

Top Left: If your engine
cuts out . . .

Top: You'll have no
plane at all.

Left: "See that village,
Corporal Bailey?" "Yes, sir,
ideal spot for a message
pick-up—dive down one
side, climb up the other."

Left: Bill King forced landed off the Needles and was drifting on to the lee shore. My Telegraphist Air Gunner managed to get a line to him and we took him in tow.

Bottom Left: Fairey Flycatcher. Carrier-borne fighter of the Fleet Air Arm.

Bottom: Fairey IIIF Seaplanes, Lee-on-the-Solent. Pilots: Middleton, Edwards, Chignell and Carr.

Right: The most elegant and swashbuckling biplane fighter of them all, the Hawker Fury. Note Squadron Commander's pennant on the fin.

Centre Right: Tony Robinson hit the ground attached to this by the shroud lines of his parachute. He lived to fly again.

Bottom: Two Ansons from Wagga collided over Albury, New South Wales, and became locked together. Three crew members bailed out, the fourth landed the two aircraft. This accident aroused world-wide interest at the time, and is unique in aviation history.

Below: Getting to town in a hurry was a very competitive business. The author's FJF special, built of bits of Bentley, bits of 30/98 Vauxhall, and bits of Bugatti. The bodywork, cockpit and instrumentation were designed for the car.

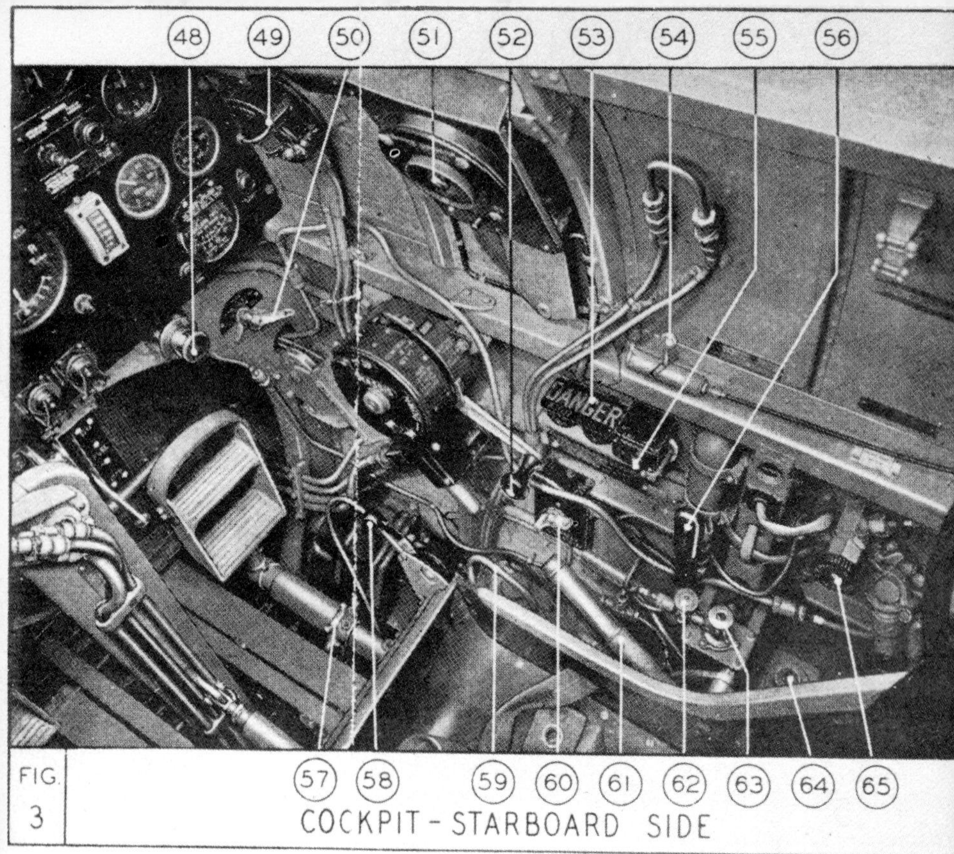

Spitfire F MkIX: instrument panel, cockpit port side, and starboard side. Instructions for use on page 128.

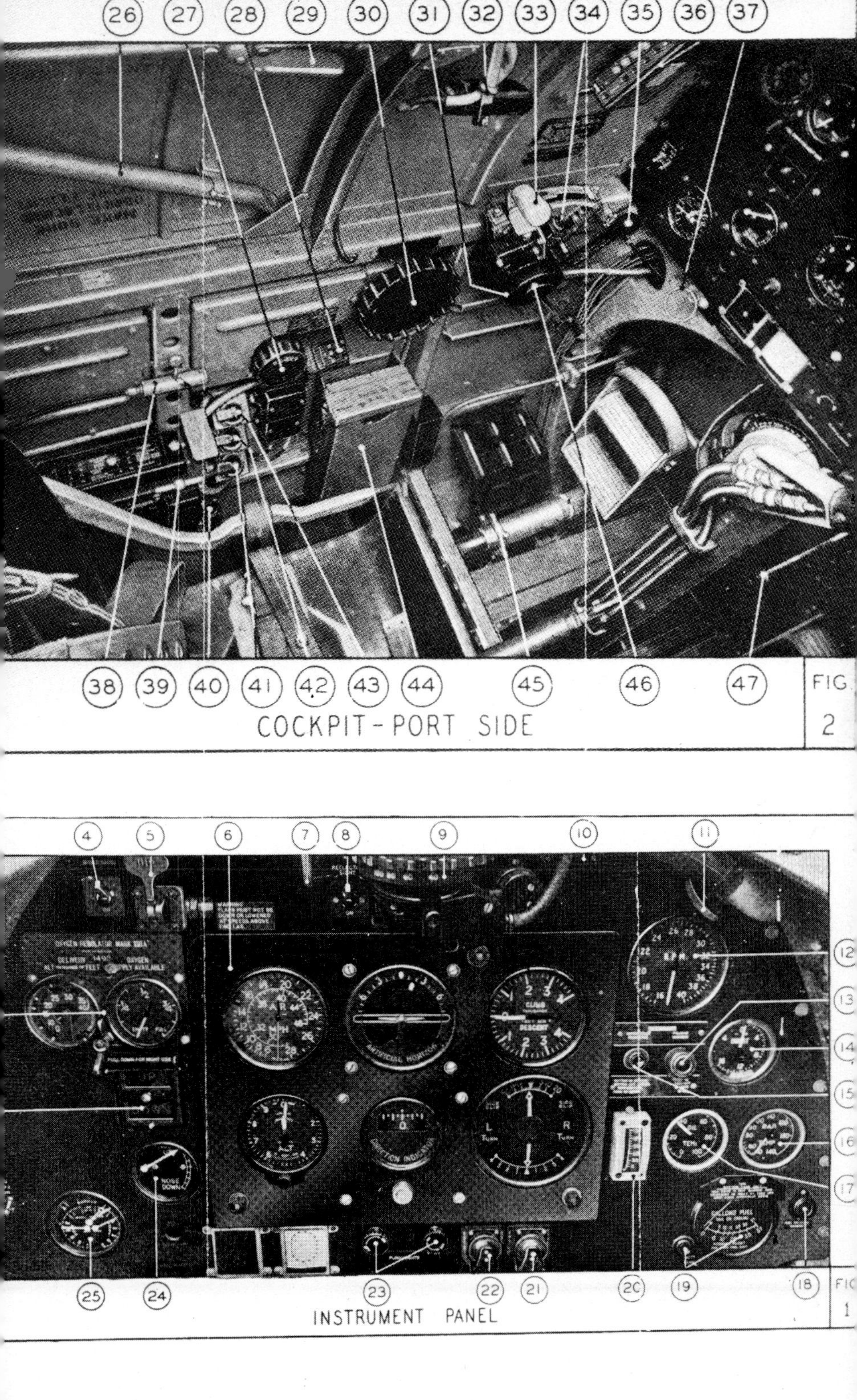

26 27 28 29 30 31 32 33 34 35 36 37
38 39 40 41 42 43 44 45 46 47
COCKPIT-PORT SIDE
FIG 2
4 5 6 7 8 9 10 11
12
13
14
15
16
17
25 24 23 22 21 20 19 18
INSTRUMENT PANEL
FIG
1

Vertical climb; Spitfire
F MkIX now owned by
Adrian Swire. It is the only
fully aerobatic Spitfire still
flying and performs regularly
at air displays.

A Tiger Moth built in 1942,
and fully restored at Rush
Green in 1973, being test-
flown by the author over
Old Warden Lake, prior to
dismantling and shipping to
the USA for its American
owner.

He answered that unfortunately the aircraft had cut his communications with Allah and he could do nothing. He told this story of a local Mullah, but as likely as not he himself was the hero of it, since they would naturally turn to him in such a case, and he has a strong sense of humour.

12. There is one further comment I should like to make. Had the circumstances been different and had there been no reason in particular why the 'Iraqi Army should have been permitted to act alone, it is still probable that I should have used a combination of land and air forces to tackle the situation, rather than attempt to conform to the purists' fanaticism by trying to do with the Air Force alone what I could do a good deal better with the Air Force co-operating with land forces.

I may be wrong but I seem to detect in your letter the suggestion that the operations ought to have been done by the Air Force alone without assistance from any ground troops. For four years at the Staff College I battled with this narrow-minded partisan attitude. In every lecture I gave, in every exercise solution and on every possible opportunity I tried to inculcate into officers of the Staff College that our object is not to devise means by which the Air Force can do without the co-operation of the other Services. This baneful influence insinuates its chill presence between the Services and lays its cold hand on every honest effort to advance the interests of inter-Service co-operation. You ought to have nothing to do with it at Andover. Your job is to study the science of the application of military force. I never have admitted and I never will admit the advantage of fighting with one hand when one can do the job more efficiently and more thoroughly with two. There are some things no doubt which can be done adequately with one hand, but why should one deny oneself the use of one's other hand simply to prove that it is possible to do without it? There may be situations in which the Air Force can do the job by itself in the most economical and efficient manner, but because of this do not let us reject the co-operation of the other Services when their help can be useful. Do not let us take up the attitude that the Air Force never requires and can never benefit by the assistance of the other services. There are many more situations in which the co-operation of land or sea forces with the Air Force is both advantageous and necessary. The Air Force can do itself nothing but harm by maintaining the contrary attitude and blowing its trumpet all by itself in the wilderness. While at the Staff College I saw fellows again and again abandon logic and common sense in their attempt to maintain claims for the Air Force which ought never to have been advanced. That is why that Pope Hennessy exercise was such a good one. I am sure the Staff College will continue to keep its energy centred on thinking out with an absolutely open and unprejudiced mind the means by which the national fighting services can best fulfil their common task of national defence without regard to the squabbles of doctrineers and partisans and their articles in service periodicals.

Yours sincerely'
(Signed) E. R. LUDLOW-HEWITT·

Of the following telegrams, the one dated 15th May 1931 from the Chief of the Air Staff to Ludlow-Hewitt is self-explanatory, but perhaps the one addressed to "Highcoma" is a bit obscure. It was from the Foreign Office on behalf of the British Government.

Secret

PARAPHRASE
A.M. 341.
Despatched Registry Telegrams 1550 15.5.31

Cipher telegram to Air Vice-Marshal Ludlow-Hewitt, Headquarters, Royal Air Force, Iraq, from Sir John Salmond, Air Ministry.

Personal
I received this morning the great news of your outstanding success. Your policy and the enterprise and determination with which it has been carried through by the Royal Air Force in your Command has brought about this result. This is yet another example of the success of air power when used as the primary arm in conjunction with troops on the ground, whose contribution of forced marches and several actions by the Iraq Army is fully realised as is also the important role played by the police.

The task of internal security of the Iraq Government when

they finally assume control should be immeasurably lightened by this surrender of a rebel leader who has been a dangerous disturber of the peace in Kurdistan for many years.

I congratulate you on the magnificent result you have achieved.

Highcoma, Baghdad.

On satisfactory conclusion of operations against Mahmud desire to express appreciation of manner in which difficult and thankless task has been carried out by Iraq Army and Police and by Royal Air Force. The successful outcome is most creditable to all concerned. Please convey congratulations of His Majesty's Government to Iraq Government and to Air Officer Commanding.

D.O. No. G.C.262
The Residency,
Baghdad.
30th April, 1931.

My dear Air Vice-Marshal,

I was very pleased to receive a letter from the Minister of the Interior expressing the 'Iraq Government's great appreciation of the gallant work of Squadron Leader G. C. Gardiner and Flying Officer S. J. Carr of 55 Squadron during the recent operations against Shaikh Mahmud.

I enclose a copy of this letter and of the report of the Inspecting Officer in Sulaimani. I should be grateful if you would communicate to these Officers the thanks of the 'Iraq Government and if you would also convey to them my own congratulations on their splendid work which has so worthily maintained the high reputation which the Royal Air Force has long enjoyed in 'Iraq.

Yours sincerely,
(Signed) F. H. Humphrys.

Air Vice-Marshal E. R. Ludlow-Hewitt,
C.B., C.M.G., D.S.O., M.C.

Oh well, it was an improvement on "incurring the grave displeasure of."

One would imagine that in the normal course of duty there would be enough excitement to satisfy every pilot in the squadron without his setting out deliberately to look for trouble, yet it was, is, and always will be possible to find something, if you are hell-bent on looking for it, which presents a challenge which you are free to accept or reject.

Such a one was the high-tension cables across the river on the outskirts of Baghdad. Flying under the cables was not in itself particularly difficult. The Tigris at this point is very wide, as a consequence of which the wires sagged tremendously in the middle of the span from their own weight, but still left room and to spare to fly underneath. If you were a bit sissy you could always fly nearer the bank, where there was less sag.

No, that bit was not difficult. The challenge lay in the fact that the cables crossed the river very close—too damned close—to the Residency where dwelt the High Commissioner, and it was expressly forbidden to fly low near the Residency for fear of alarming His Excellency.

The (self-imposed) rule therefore was that you did it without being seen by anyone on the H.C.'s staff, which called for stealth and cunning.

Normally, to get under an obstruction of this sort you would dive down with power and flatten out to fly dead straight and level just above the water, at a point far enough away to pick an aiming point and line up on it.

But you couldn't do that without alerting everybody, so instead you came over at about 2,000 feet very early in the morning, when all good citizens should still be abed. You throttled the engine right back and went into a steep engine-off dive—after all you didn't want to hang about for too long—shot under the cables, opened up to full power, stayed right down on the water, below the fairly steep river banks, so that your aircraft's serial number would not be spotted, and held it there until you were far enough away to climb.

In fact, we fooled nobody but ourselves about not being seen.

We owed our immunity from just retribution to the fact that the High Commissioner, Francis Humphrys, was a good sportsman who maintained a benevolent attitude to the young and foolhardy.

During these years the British government was taking the long view and, anticipating the time when the mandated territories could become self-governing and the British would pull out, decided that the Iraqis would, in addition to an army, need an air force of their own; so four Iraq army officers were selected for pilot training at Cranwell, and returned to Iraq in 1931. Of these four, one was posted to 55 to gain squadron and operational experience, and he was wished on to me. His name was Jenabi and he had to share my aeroplane, a circumstance which I resented and fumed over but had to accept.

As things turned out my resentment was fully justified, for he eventually turned the thing over on to its back and killed the air gunner, who suffered a broken neck. It was not, thank God, my good campaigning friend Corporal Bailey.

Even before this unfortunate tragedy there had been much muttering among the men, none of whom relished flying with these characters, and after it we very nearly had a mutiny on our hands. So very nearly, that the AOC found it necessary to address the entire squadron assembled in one of the hangars.

So that was the end of J9847. She did not go as she deserved, in a blaze of glory at the bottom of some Kurdish ravine, or splashed all over the top of a ten-thousand-foot peak half in and half out of Persia, but ignobly lay crumpled and upside-down, like a dead praying mantis, on her home airfield, with a dead air gunner underneath and the choking dust hanging like a pall in the lifeless air, and the fire tender and ambulance streaking out too late— always too late. And all because of the ham-fisted ineptitude of a misbegotten Arab, who crawled out quite unscathed.

There were compensations, or, more precisely, *a* compensation. I was issued with a brand new aircraft, K1124, straight out of its manufacturers crate, and it didn't take long to get it air tested then re-rigged to fly the way I liked an aeroplane to fly.

Jenabi was removed from the squadron and relegated to Baghdad West, the civil airport, to fiddle about in a Gipsy Moth.

One of these first four Cranwell-trained Iraqis, by then a Colonel—not Jenabi, he wouldn't have had the nous—led the insurrection against the RAF in 1940. He reckoned that Germany was going to win the war, and he wanted to be on the winning side.

Arabs, one found, did not possess the right temperament for flying. They were courageous enough when it was simply a matter of guts and fortitude, but seemed unable to acquire skill and air sense. They proved quite incapable of assessing a situation and anticipating trouble, and were therefore seldom prepared for or able to take corrective action when something went wrong.

They appear not to have changed. I have it on good authority that the Arab pilots in the air force of a certain Gulf Shaikhdom are currently taking four years to convert on to Lightnings.

It will not have escaped the reader's notice that in all references to NCOs I use their full rank: Flight Sergeant, Sergeant, Corporal, as the case may be. In the pre-war Royal Air Force it was not only customary so to address them, but it was also considered, without having to spell it out, that the rank they had earned by merit carried its own entitlement to respect.

It would not have occurred to an officer, of whatever rank, to use such terms as 'Sarge' or 'Corp'. This informal and over-familiar manner between officers and NCOs arose during World War II, partly as a result of the unavoidable practice of forming all-NCO aircrews in heavy bombers—there simply were not enough officers to be able to put one in command of every bomber—and partly because of the influence of Dominion officers and non-regulars. This situation also gave rise to the practice among Bomber Command aircrew of referring to and addressing the captain as 'Skip'.

It might be thought that in a relationship such as existed between my air gunner Corporal Bailey and me, where we flew together day after day for months on end and relied on each other in nearly every situation which confronted us, that a more relaxed attitude would have prevailed in course of time, but it never did.

We liked and respected each other, but even in moments of stress or danger—of which there was no lack—we always maintained the formality of 'Sir' and 'Corporal Bailey' (in full, not just 'Corporal') when talking through the Gosport tubes. But this did not preclude gentle leg-pulling, banter or at times, sharp criticism. In short, we were a good team.

It was time to return to UK. If you had the temerity to ask, through the proper channels of course, for a particular posting, you usually got quite the opposite, something to do with the 'exigencies of the service'. So if you asked for home-based fighters you were probably sent to Singapore or the Fleet Air Arm. It was best therefore to ask, or better still be recommended, for quite the opposite of what you wanted.

I wanted and was recommended for a flying instructor's course at CFS.

What I got was a posting to Calshot for a conversion course on to seaplanes. It must have been that chap with the pin again at Air Ministry.

CHAPTER 8

Now to Great Britain we must make our way,
Unto which Kingdom Brutus gave its name
What time he won it from the giants rule.
'Tis thought at first its name was Albion,
And Anglia, from a damsel, afterwards.
The island is so great and rich and fair,
It conquers others that in Europe be,
Even as the sun surpasses other stars.

Fazio Degli Uberti,
sixteenth century

Back in England I splashed forty pounds on a beaten-up 12/40 Alvis sports tourer, circa 1926. It had no hood, a rudimentary windscreen, minimal braking, but a lovely exhaust note and could just about do 70mph down wind.

Into this heap I loaded my all and set course for Southampton.

The finest thing about Calshot was the mess, superbly run by Mr. Swain the caterer, who ruled with a rod of iron. Messing throughout home stations in the thirties was of a very high standard and Calshot was one of the best. In most messes for breakfast there would be porridge (we hadn't yet heard of cardboard packets of roughage, and even if we had, such monstrosities would not have been permitted to sully the sideboard), kippers, smoked haddock, sausages, bacon, kidneys, eggs cooked any way you wished, all in great silver dishes on hot plates on the sideboard, and a huge ham with one of the chefs in tall hat to carve it.

There were never less than four courses for lunch, with a choice of six hot (almost always including curry for those whose palates were vitiated by too many years overseas) and an almost limitless number of cold dishes. Except on supper nights, that is, when you were not compelled to dine in, there would be a five course dinner and on guest nights always seven.

We fed like fighting cocks, all for 3/6d. per day; though of course the mess caterer drew the members' messing allowance in kind or in cash. In Iraq one had forgotten the taste of good food.

The only messes which might have been marginally better were at the CFS at Wittering, the Staff College at Andover, and those of the two London Auxiliary Squadrons at Hendon, one of which was allegedly messed by Fortnum & Masons.

Even so, we managed to grumble and the complaints book was well used, although the entries were largely facetious. But apart from the splendid mess Calshot was a shock.

With a few exceptions everybody looked a hundred years old. Some even had beards, like sailors; God damn it, some of them *were* sailors, and their jargon was as incomprehensible as Sanskrit. Out on the water, riding at their moorings, were twin-engined Saunders Roe Southampton flying boats. The thought of having to fly those ungainly-looking horrors was too depressing, but thank God they were not for me. I neither wanted to develop webbed feet nor grow a beard.

I was here to learn to fly the Fairey IIIF float-planes, built at Richard Fairey's factory at Hanworth. I was familiar with the land-plane version, there having been a number of them in the Middle East; 45 squadron had them at Helwan, as did 47 squadron at Khartoum, but I had never flown them. These were the Mark IV; the float-plane version was the Mark III, as used by the Navy.

Designed as a fleet spotter reconnaissance aircraft, it was powered by the 570hp Napier Lion liquid-cooled engine of 12 cylinders arranged in three banks of four, driving a Fairey Reed fixed-pitch metal propeller. The IIIF was a big aeroplane, with a wing span of 45ft 9in and an overall length of 34ft 4in. In the cockpit you had the feeling of sitting in the middle of a very large machine. Its performance was far from electrifying: it cruised at 100mph, reached a maximum of 120, and stalled at around 50.

The greybeards at Calshot were full of awful warnings about the inadvisability of attempting even the mildest aerobatics. They said especially that it must not be side-slipped or spun because of the enormous keel surface effect of the floats plus the long fuselage.

All of which turned out to be incorrect. You could loop, spin, stall-turn and side-slip the thing like any other aeroplane. Although it spun fast it recovered quickly, but you needed at least 1500 feet in which to effect recovery to level flight from where you stopped the spin.

The course lasted four weeks and I was posted to Lee, just across the water at the head of the Solent and slap opposite Cowes, which had certain disadvantages for a short period every summer. King George V was on the throne; he loved the Navy, but couldn't at any price stomach the RAF, which he thought was a wild undisciplined bunch of thugs. He could have been right. As Commodore of the Royal Yacht Squadron he was always there during Cowes week, and no aircraft were permitted to befoul the sky within five miles of Cowes during that week, which made things awkward at Lee, since it was only about that distance away in any case. It was one rule none of us dared to break.

It is possible that one can grow to like almost any aeroplane, though I can think of some I never fell in love with, but the IIIF claimed affection of a sort from most of those who flew it, with one notable exception. Colonel Charles Lindbergh flew one during a visit to England and reported as follows:

'A cavernous cockpit filled with nothing but smell and noise and me, supported by great shuddering wings strung together by random struts and wire and string. The engine sounded somehow as if it had been running since the beginning of time but that it would go on till the end.'

Once in the air a twin-float seaplane handles like any other aeroplane and the only thing one needed to learn all over again was the take-off and landing, during both of which the fore and aft movements of the stick were almost exactly the reverse of land-plane technique. Instead of shoving the stick forward to get the tail up, you held it hard back to begin with, to get the toes of the floats clear of the water. You pushed the stick forward to get her up on to the step—that is, in the hydroplaning attitude—and then, as flying speed was reached, eased gently back and she would come off nicely. A choppy sea was the ideal water condition, since it allowed air to get under the step. It took a long run to unstick in a flat calm.

Landing presented no problem; you put the aircraft on to the water in a slightly tail-down attitude and as the speed dropped off you hauled the stick hard back into your guts. Again, this was to hold the toe of the floats well up, otherwise, especially in a rough sea, they could dig in and the whole outfit could turn over on its back.

As speed was lost she would gently adopt a naturally horizontal floating attitude, but landing on a flat glassy calm was a hazard because of the difficulty of judging height. This problem was accentuated in clear shallow water because in such conditions you could often see the bottom, which might be twenty or thirty feet down, but could seldom gauge the actual surface, and the danger here was of flying straight into the drink without holding off.

To overcome this difficulty, it was usual to have a line of buoys, strung out like a flare path, by which to judge height. Alternatively, since a flat calm denoted no wind, you could land parallel and close into the shore, looking at the beach instead of the water.

Unlike flying boats, which stayed out at moorings all the time, a float plane, being more vulnerable to rough seas and high winds, had to be brought up the slipway and into the hangars. For this beaching a trolley was fixed to the floats and a winch cable hooked on to it to haul the aircraft up the slipway. This was the job of the waders; airmen and sailors who spent most of the day up to their armpits in water. All right in the summer but not very jolly in winter. They got a daily rum ration but could opt for 2d a day in lieu if they were teetotal.

It called for careful judgement of taxiing speed, wind, tide and drift in order to choose the right moment to switch off as you approached the slip. If you cut the engine too soon, especially with an offshore wind, the waders would be out of their depth before they could reach the aircraft with the winch wire and the trolley; and there you would be, alone in your idiotic predicament and drifting out of control back to sea, for there was no other way of restarting the engine than by the standard method of two men, one each side of the engine nacelle, winding away with the starting handles.

If you left it too late before cutting the switches you would clout the concrete slipway, to the detriment of the floats, and be in grave danger of decapitating one of the waders with that great big spinning metal prop.

The unkindest task of any allotted to a Fairey IIIF, and indeed to a pilot, was the indignity of target towing for gunnery practice which, with a large piece of canvas flapping about at the end of four hundred yards of steel cable, reduced the speed to a bare eighty mph.

The winch was located behind the pilot's cockpit and was driven by a large four-bladed windmill sticking out into the slipstream on the starboard side.

Unless some very lucky shot severed the cable early in the

exercise the poor wretched pilot could be flogging up and down the gunnery area for five hours at a stretch.

Fortunately for all the pilots bar one, this thankless chore was performed by a separate little lodger unit at Lee-on-Solent.

The pilot in question habitually wore a voluminous woollen scarf, the two ends of which fluttered out behind him in the slipstream. On one occasion the ends of the scarf got entangled with the winch wire and wrapped themselves around the cable drum, inexorably yanking the pilot out of the cockpit and coming close to strangling him to death. The winch operator, a sailor, was equipped as all sailors are with a great big jack-knife, and resourceful as always hacked through the scarf with lightning speed and freed the pilot, who recovered his breath and his senses just in time to regain control and prevent the IIIF from plunging into the sea. He never wore a scarf again.

Shortly after, but not as a result of this incident, the infant science of radio remote control had made sufficient strides to justify a more sophisticated approach to providing airborne gunnery targets.

This was the Fairie Queen radio-controlled target aircraft with automatic pilot, which in the fulness of time, since it was an expensive business shooting down IIIFs, was replaced by similarly modified and adapted Tiger Moths, known as Queen Bees. No relation to senior WAAF officers.

Compared with Iraq the flying at Lee was excessively dull.

The School of Naval Co-operation, to give it its full title, existed to train Fleet Air Arm officers as observers, and naval ratings as telegraphist air gunners. The course was six months, at the end of which, after a suitable interval for leave, the whole monotonous cycle began all over again.

The observers did all the real work of navigation, spotting, practice bombing, reconnaissance and so on, while the pilot concentrated on flying very accurate compass courses. All you ever saw was the sea, the sky and ships.

We may not have had much of an air force in the mid thirties, but we certainly had a navy. Great battleships and battle cruisers such as *Nelson*, *Rodney*, *Valiant*, *Hood*, *Barham*, *Howe* and *Warspite*, aircraft carriers such as *Courageous*, *Furious*, *Glorious*, *Argus*, *Hermes* and *Eagle*, and the heavy cruisers *York*, *Exeter*, *Norfolk* and *Dorsetshire*, whose catapult seaplanes used Lee-on-

Solent as their shore station when the vessels were in port; and fussing around these great warships, like sheep dogs at a cattle market and just as cheeky and audacious, were destroyers by the score.

You could relieve the tedium at the end of the exercise by landing, if sea conditions were suitable, alongside some great Cunarder, or perhaps the *Bremen* or *Île de France*, as they were steaming up the Solent, and taxiing alongside wave to all the girls lined up along the rail. Better still, you could go for a good old low-flying beat-up all along the coast to Brighton and back, to give the holidaymakers a treat.

If there was a small boat regatta at Ventnor or some such place, we thought it terribly funny to fly flat out right down on the water and blow them over with our slip-stream.

Most of the fun at Lee had nothing to do with flying, but it did produce moments of high comedy.

Twice a year a bunch of Admirals and Post Captains arrived from the Senior Officers' tactical course at Portsmouth for air experience. Few of them had ever flown and they didn't know what it was all about. No doubt they were destined to command aircraft carriers.

Bill King, who weighed seventeen stone and drank a bottle of whisky a day (he retired from rugby football at nineteen), was not the best of pilots; his flying somewhat lacked finesse. He drew an admiral as passenger.

There was an off-shore wind and on returning to base Bill decided to do a slipway landing. We all liked doing this. There were not many ways in which you could be split-arse with a sea-plane, but this was one of them. The idea was to approach straight towards the slipway and touch down at a point which would enable you to complete the landing run with engine switched off just short of the slip, so that the aircraft would very gently touch bottom and be grabbed by the waders.

It called for good judgement and precise attention to approach speed, strength of wind and condition of sea.

Bill came in at a good 100mph, touched down about fifty yards from shore, still going like a bat out of hell, bounced straight out of the water, shot up the slipway with sparks flying from the floats, crossed the road and shuddered to a standstill on the parade ground right in front of the hangars.

The Admiral climbed out beaming, patted Bill on the shoulder, thanked him warmly and trundled away to the white-faced reception party, firmly convinced that this was how seaplanes were always landed. Nobody disillusioned him.

Another admiral figured frequently in our lives, but indirectly. He had a splendid house in a village a few miles along the coast, and two daughters who spent most of the summer in or alongside their swimming pool in the middle of a vast lawn. The girls had got aircraft recognition down to a fine art and could have taught the Observer Corps a thing or two. They also had a very comprehensive set of ground strip signals. So no matter what sort of aeroplane you were flying, if you happened, just by chance of course, to be anywhere near that certain village, you would see down there on the lawn a signal: "Hello, Flycatcher, please stunt", or "Hello Osprey", or "Hello, IIIF, please stunt." Now tell me how any young RAF pilot of pre-war days could resist an invitation like that, despite the fact that the most popular way of killing yourself in the thirties was by showing off to some girl or other with a fine display of low-level aerobatics.

Notwithstanding that seaplanes were not allowed to fly over land other than at an altitude which would enable them to reach open water in the event of engine failure, ' Hello IIIF, please stunt" was not to be ignored; so there you were again, up to no good and risking court-martial.

A few days later there would be a message via one of the mess stewards. Would the officer who was flying Fairey IIIF S1502 (they always got the serial number) over Blank at 3.00pm on such and such a day kindly telephone Blank 1234? So you did just that. It was Mrs Admiral, to enquire if you would care to dine one evening. I have no idea who the girls married in the end, but they sure did work hard at it.

But what made Lee such a three-ring circus was not the flying but the people. If I had thought the squadrons in Iraq were full of characters, with a smattering of near-lunatics, it was only because my experience was limited. The School of Naval Co-operation was equally well blessed, as indeed was the entire Royal Air Force. The service was so small that it did not take many years to get to know very nearly everyone in it.

In 1934 the entire strength of the RAF was 32,000, of which only 1,700 were officers, and it was impossible to walk into any mess anywhere in the world without meeting at least one man you knew, and those you hadn't met you knew by name and reputation, good or bad. The service in fact was one great big flying club—the best in the world—which is really what it was about for most people. Nobody joined for the money. A pilot officer, on confirmation in rank, was paid twelve shillings a day. A flying officer, on appointment, got eighteen shillings, and after two years seniority in his rank received the staggering sum of one pound and six pence, six shillings of which was called 'flying pay' or 'danger money'. Six bob a day for risking your silly neck. I was once (once?) on the carpet for some misdemeanour or other, and the CO asked what my daily rate of pay was (as if he didn't know). "One pound and six pence," I said brightly. "Yes," said he, "you are paid six pence for the work you do and a pound to use your initiative whenever the need arises. Go away and think about it."

To return to the characters. There was O'Grady. I ran into him on the Sunday night of my arrival at Lee. It was standard practice to report to a new unit on a Monday, so one invariably arrived as late as possible on Sunday night. There was always a duty mess steward to show you to your room.

The ante-room was lit, so I walked in. All those great big old service issue green leather sofas and armchairs were lying face down on the floor and there was this red-headed character on his hands and knees, feeling round the back and down the sides of the cushions.

"Hello chaps," I said. "What are you doing?"

"Hello old boy, are you the new arrival? Well, it's like this. All the springs have gone in this junk and when you sit down your bum is about two feet lower than your knees, consequently the loose cash in your trouser pockets slips out and goes down the back. I always wait till everyone has gone to bed and then do the rounds. I sometimes collect quite a haul."

O'Grady had a fat amiable Sealyham which he took with him everywhere, but especially to a certain tea shop in Southampton much frequented by the local girls. He'd trained this damn dog to go to any table occupied by one or two girls, sit up on its haunches with a sad face and beg. The girls couldn't resist it. He would then stroll over, give the dog a rocket and apologise in a great imitation of an Irish brogue. It never failed.

Almost every member of the mess had a dog, or dogs, and despite 'Rules for the Conduct of Officers Messes' all of them were allowed in the ante-room, which caused chaos on many occasions. One man had a huge Great Dane bitch which never did become house-trained. It left great pools you could drown in all over the place. Chignell's Border terriers were always fighting Kelly's Kerry Blue. Someone else's Bull terrier killed the adjutant's cat. The ante-room was a permanent shambles. Not only because of dogs. If you were sitting quietly reading *The Times*, holding up its full spread in front of your face, more often than not it would shortly burst into flames because some ass had put a match to it. You then flung it from you in terror, whereupon it promptly set fire to the chair into which it had fallen. Then naturally someone would rush in with a foam fire-extinguisher and squirt that all over the place. Not for nothing was it called the officers' mess.

On every guest night without fail the adjutant was flung into the goldfish pond in his mess kit; he thought it was because he was popular.

We used to play these terrible games after dinner, one of which was a competition to see who could dive head-first across the greatest number of chairs and sofas placed back to back. You took the longest possible run and just launched yourself. Two stalwart characters were posted to catch you before you hit the ground. Everyone had had a go except the adjutant. Shouting "My turn!" he hurled himself through the air. Chignell and Lulu Louden were doing the catching and, seeing who it was, said "Nuts", or something similar, and walked away.

We got on with the next thing, which was probably hi-cock-a-lorum or going right round the ante-room without touching the floor. About two hours later somebody said, "Where's the adjutant? It's time he went in the pond", but he hadn't been seen since the chair-diving, so we went to look, and there he was, unconscious. The poor chap had broken his neck, but fortunately he wasn't dead and did eventually fully recover, though he had a wry neck from then on.

The station armament officer was a dull middle-aged flight lieutenant, formerly a Naval Warrant Officer and known as a 'one-three-eighter', from the Admiralty order number 138, which promoted a number of men from the lower deck to limited career commissions. He was a decent stick but quite humourless, and therefore a natural butt for what passed for wit among the younger members. He too always suffered the same fate on the monthly guest night, which was to be de-bagged and held down by half a dozen young ruffians while another, usually Johnny Dewar, burnt his bush off with matches. It had always grown just enough to make it worthwhile doing a month later.

Finally he decided he would not suffer this indignity again, and immediately the President rose from his chair, to indicate that members who wished to could leave the table, the 'one-three-eighter' tore off to his room and locked himself in. It took more than a locked door to deter Johnny Dewar, who incidentally got one of the first DFCs in the last war but was shot down in flames (poetic justice?) a few weeks later. He rushed down to his car, came back with a two-gallon can of petrol, sloshed a fair dollop of it on the floor, set fire to it, seized the fire bucket off the corridor wall and floated the burning petrol under the poor chap's door. He opened up in a panic, was seized, carted bodily down to the ante-room, debagged and had his bush burnt off. After which he asked for, and obtained, a posting.

Guest nights were always cluttered up with VIPs, such as C-in-C Home Fleet, GOC Southern District, AOC Coastal Area, the Lord Mayor of Portsmouth, old Uncle Tom Cobbley and all. Naturally we waited until they had all gone home to their wives and beds before starting any nonsense.

One night however, the station commander, who liked his brandy, and the C-in-C, Howard Kelly, just would not go. They stood with their backs to the fire toasting their behinds for hours on end. Johnny Dewar volunteered to shift them. We all went outside quietly and unostentatiously, two or three at a time. Johnny went down to flying control (it was called the watch hut then) and came back with a rocket signal flare Mark III. He proposed to crawl into the ante-room on hands and knees, creep up behind the C-in-C and stuff the rocket up the chimney, leaving the fire to do the igniting part. Whether the two were so engrossed in each other's yarns or whether it was the brandy, who can say, but while we watched through the windows from out in the garden, sure enough in crawled Johnny, placed the rocket and crawled out again. The rocket shot up the chimney with a roar. Great billowing clouds of black smoke and soot blotted the scene from our goggling eyes and two very senior officers rushed gasping out of the front door looking for all the world like nigger minstrels. We went back into the mess when the atmosphere had cleared and had a party. We never heard another word about it, which was typical of Howard Kelly. He was a sailor's sailor; an airman's sailor too, for that matter. It was he who, when King George V reviewed the fleet at Spithead, sent the signal 'Pro Bono Publico no ruddy Panico'.

Try as we may, we never succeeded in burning down the mess, not even on the night we fought a Very pistol battle with our naval mess-mates. The ante-room had three outside walls with long rows of windows on each side. The Navy took station on one side, the RAF on the other, and on the command "let battle commence!", we let fly with the Very cartridges through the windows, across the room and, we hoped, out the other side. I once saw a man shot in the guts at close range with a Very cartridge. It was a very messy way to die.

On another occasion, Guy Fawkes night, we had a horizontal rocket-firing competition. There was a long wide corridor leading from the front hall, the walls of which were lined with rows and rows of framed photographs of previous courses and of senior officers of both services. E.C.T. Edwards, Oxford rowing blue and most skilful of pilots, who was killed early in the war, organised a contest to see who could knock most pictures off the wall with a rocket. It was a great success; the place was ankle deep in broken glass and burning carpet, and while all this was going on Slocum climbed on to the roof and fired Very lights down all the chimneys. It was one of the better guest nights.

Slocum was an odd character whose life was dedicated to defying authority. Good-looking in a tough broken-nosed sort of way, he was inter-services officers' welterweight champion, right wing threequarter for Richmond and capped half a dozen times for the RAF. (These were the years of the RAF's ascendancy in rugby football, the years of W.W. Wakefield's captaincy, of the Beamish brothers, George, Victor and Francis, of Bill Williams, Gus Walker, Connie Constantine and Jock MacLean.) Slocum, like so many boxers, affected a bizarre taste in clothes. Even in uniform he would not conform. He often used to come on parade in suede shoes and a teddy-bear camel coat, because he had lost his great-coat, and he always wore his fore-and-aft cap slanted to the left instead of the regulation right; when remonstrated with by a senior officer he replied, "I prefer it like this, sir" and got away with it. He was a most alarming character to go out with. It always ended in trouble. His idea of an evening's entertainment was a tour of the sailors' pubs in Portsmouth.

Wearing a black beret, black and white co-respondent shoes, a black and white dog-tooth check suit and a black shirt with a black and white bow tie, he would mince up to the bar among all the ABs and chief petty officer stokers and, pretending to be a queer, ask for a sherry and egg "for my friend" and a port and lemon, or something equally nauseating, for himself, then wait for it to happen. It always did. The matelots couldn't resist it.

There would be winks and elbow nudgings, and a sailor or two would make some snide remark, or maybe just sort of accidentally make Slocum spill his drink. As quick as lightning out would snake that left, then a quick right hook, and one or more often two great big ABs were flat on their backs in the sawdust, out for the count. The look of utter consternation on the faces of the others was worth a guinea a minute. Then Slocum would calmly finish his drink, call for further volunteers—there never were any—step over the recumbent bodies and go and repeat the performance in the next pub.

He had a girl-friend who lived at Micheldever. She was a trick cyclist on the music halls and married to an American all-in wrestler who was in the States, and we all waited for the day when he walked back in and caught Slocum with his pants down.

He never even remained on station when he was orderly officer, but would get changed at around 6pm, ask some other character too broke to go out if he would turn out the guard at 2200hrs, then would climb into his red Austro Daimler, with its wire wheels, flared wings and outside exhaust, and roar off to Micheldever.

Even the way he died was in character. In the early days of the war he was flying a Hudson painted in an experimental camouflage, and was mistaken for an enemy aircraft by three Hurricanes over the Thames estuary. They shot him down. All his crew bailed out safely, but not Slocum, who hadn't got a parachute—"Can't be bothered with the damn thing, old boy."

But if the junior officers of both services were a wild undisciplined irresponsible bunch of overgrown schoolboys, the group captain commanding was very little better, though in his case it was quite unintentional. It will not do to identify him, beyond mentioning that he was as rich as Croesus and his wife even more so.

A splendid mixture of Mrs. Malaprop and the Reverend Mr. Spooner, he was always plaiting his words, even when not excited. Consequently his commands were usually unintelligible, and since it suited us to misinterpret his intentions anyway, the shambles that ensued whenever he took a parade had to be seen to be believed. By the time one flight had almost disappeared off the parade ground and another was marching down the slipway into the sea, he had completely forgotten that the only command left to him was "Halt!" At this point the adjutant, with admirable tact, would salute smartly and ask, "Permission to carry on, sir?"

It was really the CO's fault that Lee-on-the-Solent pier was destroyed. It was a long pier with nothing much on it except a theatre-cum-dance hall at the far end, which one night caught fire. Not surprisingly, in view of the incendiary tendencies of the junior officers, we had a well-organised and highly efficient fire fighting section on the station and, being much nearer, were on the scene and in action long before the local fire brigades. In no time we had our hoses laid out all along the deck of the pier and two fine jets of water playing on the fire. At this point along came the station commander, full of enthusiasm, yelling "Fire break, fire break, we must have a fire break." Somewhere in the recesses of his mind he'd stored some knowledge pertaining to forest fires.

"A what, sir?" we said.

"A fire break; get out the axes and check through the dopp, I mean, chop through the deck."

So out came the axes and within seconds some enthusiast had chopped both hoses in half. There was nothing more we could do. By the time the Gosport, Fareham and Portsmouth brigades arrived the end of the pier had burnt down to the water line.

He successfully demolished another building. The ration store was a World War I wooden barrack hut with no foundations, and it was infested with rats.

I was requested to report to the commanding officer.

"Ah, crying officer Farr, what do you want to see me about?"

"I don't, sir, you sent for *me*."

"Oh yes, of course. I have appointed you the Peed Piper of Hamlet."

"The what, sir? . . . Oh, you meant the Pied . . ."

"Yes, as I said, the Pied Peeper of Hamleys. The rats, Carr, the rats, we've got to get rid of the rats."

"Good idea, sir, we can borrow some ferrets and use the terriers. Have a bit of fun."

"No, you will not have fun. There will be no terrets and no ferriers. You will give the fire section some practice. Rush the flats out from under, with hoses you understand. Go and write an appreciation of the situation—courses of action, character of the enemy commander, all that sort of thing. Might be useful if you ever go to the staff college. Follow it up with an operation order."

He was so wrong about us not having any fun. It was a riot. The ground beneath the hut was soft and honeycombed with rat runs. The high pressure jets did a splendid job of earth moving and in less than an hour the ration store wasn't a store any more. It didn't go dramatically with a splintering crash, it just gently subsided at one corner then slowly fell over, with a sort of sigh. The rats merely went somewhere else.

Even the medical officer was more than a little eccentric. The Royal Air Force must have been short of doctors at the time, because this one was well past seventy and had retired some years previously from the Indian Army, with which he had been stuck for fifty years somewhere up the Khyber.

He hadn't progressed much beyond rum as an anaesthetic and hot tar to slap on the end of the amputated leg.

It was not customary for the wives and families of married men to report to sick quarters. Instead the MO did a routine daily tour of married quarters. One day an agitated sergeant requested permission to see the adjutant. He wished to complain about the MO.

"What about the MO, sergeant?"

"He's upset my wife, sir. She don't like his language."

"I see. What did he say?"

"Well, sir, she's got a boil on her behind, and he said 'all right, missus, take your drawers off, cock yer arse up on the table and let's have a look at it.' She thinks it's not the proper way to speak to a lady, sir."

One might imagine that among all these harebrained people there would be at least one ordinary normal standard-pattern individual, and indeed you might justifiably expect it to be the padre; this may have been the case almost anywhere else, but not at Lee-on-the-Solent.

A certain roistering, womanising flying officer named—well, let's call him Priest—was on a short service commission and about to be transferred to reserve.

"In a year's time," he said, "I'll be back as a squadron leader."

"Rubbish," we said. "Go away."

So Flying Officer Priest went away, did a year at a theological college, was ordained, applied to Air Ministry for a chaplaincy, got it, and was posted to the School of Naval Co-operation.

Padres in the RAF begin their careers dressed as squadron leaders.

There were others: Miles de'L, who marched up and down the corridors half the night, practising his blasted bagpipes; the chap who used to lie on his bed and shoot at flies on the ceiling with a .22 pistol; and Willie Wilson, who could never get to town fast enough every weekend. He could have got to town fast enough if he had waited a few years, for the next time we served together, at Farnborough, Willie was testing the Gloster Twin, the prototype of the Meteor, the first RAF jet fighter, and he was the first man ever to exceed 600mph in level flight.

Getting to town in a hurry was a highly competitive exercise. Motoring in the thirties was almost as much fun as flying, since other than in and around large towns the roads were empty, apart from the occasional overbodied and underpowered family saloon, none of which ever seemed to exceed forty mph down hill. So despite the narrow twisting roads it was possible to put up very high average speeds in the sports cars of the day.

Lee-on-the-Solent had the usual equipment, such as could be seen outside any RAF mess: Bentleys, Alvises, Lagondas, MGs, 30/98 Vauxhalls (Casper John, who became First Sea Lord, had one of those), Brooklands Rileys and the occasional exotic, such as a Delahaye or Bugatti, or if you were very rich, a Hispano Suiza—all second hand of course. If you were a long way from being very rich you had a bull-nosed Morris Cowley. The rivalry was in trying to break the Portsmouth (Hard) to London (Hyde Park Corner) record, which finally fell to Glen Kidston of the Navy, who did it in fifty minutes driving a blown 36/220 Mercedes. The record still stands and is unlikely ever to be beaten, unless somebody builds a motorway from Hyde Park Corner to Portsmouth Hard.

It would be improper to refer to the services and their close association with Portsmouth, Gosport and Lee-on-the-Solent without mentioning Gieves on Portsmouth Hard. Gieves were not just any old military tailors. They were an institution. Not only did they make uniforms for the three services, especially for the Navy (which they had been doing since 1730), but they were also first-class civilian tailors who ensured that you were correctly dressed for every social occasion. It mattered not whether you hunted, shot, fished, played polo, sailed, skied, climbed mountains, or all of these things, or merely spent your spare time poodle faking, Gieves would see to it that you were properly turned out. They would hire you a full dress uniform if you were bidden to a levee, and provide a diamond tiara and three feathers for your wife if she was to be 'presented'. Nor was that all. If you ran out of money—because the banks were closed of course, not because you were hard up—they would lend you a fiver or tenner and put it on the bill.

Nobody, I believe, ever paid for anything outright. Instead you signed a banker's order for so much a month and then forgot about it. People often remained in debt to Gieves up to and beyond retiring age, from Snotty to Admiral and Pilot Officer to Air Marshal.

On one occasion a destroyer entered harbour to pay off at the end of a commission, but came alongside too late for the paymaster to get money for the purpose. To hold all the ratings on board till the following day, when all they could think about after two years on the China station was getting back to wives and girl friends, was unthinkable, so the paymaster armed himself with two kitbags, stepped ashore and into Gieves and borrowed several thousand pounds in notes, silver and copper to pay off the ship's company.

But the nicest story I know about Gieves concerns a young N.O., who was up before the beak for a motoring offence.

Johnny Gieve was on the bench. Chairman no less, and after hearing all the evidence and conferring with his fellow magistrates, he rapped the table and said "Fined five pounds".

The N.O., rattling the two half-crowns in his pocket, said "Put it on my bill."

"And five pounds for contempt of court," said Gieve.

"Well, you'll have to put that on the bill too."

And he did.

CHAPTER 9

It's circuits and bumps from morning to noon
And instrument flying till tea
Hold her off, give her bank, put your undercart down
You're skidding, you're slipping, that's me.

And as soon as you've finished with one course
Like a flash up another one bobs
And there's four more to shew round the cockpit
And four more to try out the knobs.

A. P. Herbert, 'The Instructor's Lament'

Nothing lasts for ever, not even flying obsolete seaplanes. A whole new family of exciting aeroplanes were in the air: the Hawker Hart with its derivatives Hind, Audax, Demon and Osprey and that most lovely and elegant of all biplane fighters from the same factory, the Fury, already replacing Siskins and Bulldogs in the squadrons. At last I got the hoped-for instructors' course.

It was time to stop playing the fool and grow up; instructors, one understood, were expected to set an example on the ground as well as in the air. One wondered who was fooling whom.

The old Avro 504 had gone; the aeroplanes on which we were taught to instruct were the Cadet and the Tutor, but still from A. V. Roe. They were quite delightful after the great lumpy old Fairey IIIF and of the two I preferred the Cadet, such a lively and sensitive little aeroplane, which responded to the most delicate pressure on the controls. It had the Armstrong Siddeley Genet radial engine, whereas the Tutor, a slightly bigger aircraft, had the more powerful Lynx. It also had an inverted fuel system so that you could fly inverted for as long as you personally could stand being upside down.

It was a joy at last to be able to perform real aerobatics; but I wonder why anybody imagined that flying instructors were sedate.

At CFS there was a daily instructors' half-hour first thing every morning, during which no aeroplane was the right way up except when taking off and landing and no aeroplane was at a greater height than one hundred feet.

The final part of my passing out test—D'Arcy Grieg was chief flying instructor at the time—after we had finished the patter bit in a Tutor, was to demonstrate my aerobatic prowess in a Fury.

I had never previously flown one. We climbed out of the Tutor and D'Arcy said:

"See that Fury?"

"Yes."

"Right, take it off. Aerobat it over the aerodrome, everything you know, nothing over 500 feet. I'll be standing here watching."

Imagine anyone giving an order like that today.

With 1400 hours solo in your log book you probably thought of yourself as a pretty competent pilot, if you thought about it at all —which in fact you didn't.

Flying was your profession and you took it for granted.

What an instructors' course revealed was that although your competence and skill might not be in doubt you had, over the years, become casual, had developed some bad habits and allowed your flying to become at times imprecise, if not downright sloppy. Probably only in small things, which from a safety angle were not significant. For example, the correct approach speed for a landing on a given aircraft might be say 65 knots, but you didn't really bother your head if you were bringing it in at 62 or 68. In the latter case you swish-tailed the aeroplane a few times to kill the speed when you were near the ground (I refer to pre-flap days), and in the other case you rounded out the landing a bit quicker by moving the stick back a shade faster.

It normally didn't matter one way or the other, but it mattered a very great deal when you were teaching someone to fly. The patter, that is, the words you spoke to the pupil through the Gosport tubes, had to be exactly synchronised with what the aeroplane was doing at any given moment—so if you were demonstrating an approach and landing it was no good saying, "Close the throttle at 700 feet and adjust the tail trim to glide at 65 knots", if in fact a glance at the instruments revealed that you had closed the throttle when the altimeter registered 600 feet and the airspeed indicator was reading 70 knots. Even the dimmest pupil might surmise that things were not what they purported to be. Equally with the landing itself.

It would be an unconvincing demonstration to say, "Hold the aircraft about a foot above the ground by gentle backward pressure on the stick, gradually increasing the rate of backward movement until, with the stick right back in your tummy, the aircraft stalls and sinks gently on to the ground, wheels and tail skid together", if you were still talking ten seconds after the aeroplane had landed, or it was still flying ten seconds after you had finished your little chat, or worse still you had held off at ten feet and let it fall on to the ground with a crunch.

In short, you had to eradicate the slapdash methods which had served you well enough in the past and get down to the exacting business of 100% precision flying, because although a pilot is never an ace to his airgunner, an instructor is always a demi-god to his pupil.

At one stage during my long, long stint as a flying instructor I was at the elementary and reserve flying school at Filton, operated by the Bristol Aeroplane Company under contract to the Air Ministry. This was fun because the flying instructors also did all the production test piloting for the company.

This was not confined to aircraft of the company's own design and construction but, because Bristols were among the leading makers of aero engines, included aircraft from pretty well every manufacturer in the country, most of which were used at Filton as engine test-beds.

The company's own aircraft, at any rate the single-engined ones, were always nice to fly. The Bulldog for example, though my own favourite was a SS fighter which never went into RAF service. This was the Bullpup, smaller overall than the Bulldog but with more power, having the experimental Aquila sleeve valve nine-cylinder radial. It was in this aircraft that I reached the highest altitude I had ever attempted without oxygen, 23,000 feet.

I was doing a high rate of climb, high rate of descent series of tests at different flight levels from five thousand to as high as I could get, to test the effect of rapid heating and cooling on the exhaust system. Nothing remarkable about this, and I only mention it to illustrate the odd effects of anoxia.

I had to make notes on my knee pad of cylinder-head temperatures, exhaust collector ring temperatures, boost pressures and so on, and thought I was doing a marvellous job, until I got back on to the ground and discovered that my notes and comments from fifteen thousand feet up were complete gibberish.

We flew the Gloster Gauntlet (forerunner of the Gladiator),

Hawker Harts and Hart variants, with various marks of Pegasus engines, and also conventionally-engined aircraft—that is to say, those having the engine for which they were designed (e.g. the Fury with the Rolls Royce Kestrel)—in comparative trials and so on.

It was quite revealing how the individual types from each maker had flying characteristics similar to all that maker's other aircraft. Some, as was the case with Hawker aircraft, handled as a thoroughbred horse would handle, while others, such as those from A. V. Roe, would provide a nice gentlemanly trouble-free ride, like a well-schooled hunter. Aeroplanes from Glosters were more like a polo pony—turn on a sixpence—while those from some other makers were akin to a farmer's cob, stodgy but reliable —get you home dead drunk from market. There were even some carthorses, but I don't want to hurt anybody's feelings by naming names, and also a few mules, vicious and unpredictable—kick you in the pants the minute your attention wandered. But more even than the designer, a company's chief test-pilot stamped his personality on the product. Men like George Bulman of Hawkers, Chris Staniland of Faireys, Geoffrey de Haviland of de Havilands, Cyril Uwins of Bristols, Gerry Sayers of Glosters, and many more.

But the bread-and-butter aeroplane, the one in which all the instruction took place, was the ubiquitous Tiger Moth which with its 130hp Gipsy Major engine was cheap to operate compared with contemporary trainers, and sufficiently unstable and sensitive on the controls to make it a very good aeroplane on which to learn to fly.

It was almost impossible to trim a Tiger to fly hands-off, even in the calmest air, so that it had to be consciously flown all the time, and although the landing was quite straightforward, it was not easy for the novice to achieve a good three-point landing without making a determined effort. It was therefore not only a good trainer but also made the transition to heavier, faster and more sophisticated aircraft less traumatic than might otherwise be the case. Witness of the de Haviland Tiger Moth's excellence is the fact that more pilots were trained on it than on any other type ever produced.

It was used throughout the last war in every Commonwealth air force and most other countries.

Up to 1939 some 1424 Tiger Moths had been built, and by

1945 the grand total stood in excess of 9000. There are now no more than thirty still flying in the United Kingdom.

A trick used to be played by instructors on pupils who were finding the going difficult and were lacking in confidence; the instructor would have a spare control column in the front cockpit, and in a fit of simulated exasperation he would wave it in the air then, with suitable expressions of disgust, fling it over the side, saying, "Now, either fly the damned aeroplane or kill us both."

This trick was hoary with age. It had been done to death.

But John Arbuthnot perpetrated a much modified form of it quite unintentionally. John was a delightfully vague character and really not of this world at all.

His pupil had progressed to the point where he could do an acceptable take-off and circuit but had still a long way to go with his landings.

John climbed into the front seat, strapped himself in and said, "OK, you have control, taxi out and take off." Half-way round the circuit he said, "All right, I've got her. I'll do the first landing and I want you to follow me through on the controls." Reaching for the stick, he discovered to his horror that he hadn't got one. The aircraft's previous flight had been solo, for which it was standard procedure to remove the front control column so that it could not be fouled by the Sutton harness.

With complete calm, John said, "No, on second thoughts, I would like you to land the aircraft, and I want to see if you can do it without me having to touch the stick," and he talked the boy down to what was probably the best landing he was ever likely to make.

My Filton days came to an end in the fulness of time and were followed by appointments at other flying training establishments, in various capacities, including that of CFI. None was especially remarkable, though the most enjoyable was a spell in Scotland. Because of the shooting rather than the flying.

Scotland is a shooting and fishing man's paradise. I once had the shooting rights over a wild and remote area of about 1000 acres up in the hills halfway between Blairgowrie and Kirkmichael. It consisted of moorland, bog, rough grazing and some low ground scrub, and was dominated by a heather-clad hill called a 'knock' right in the middle. It was not the sort of place on which to stage a formal day of seven or eight guns with beaters, but was essentially a rough shoot where one, or at most two, with one or more good dogs, could have a really pleasant day of hard walking and intriguing sport.

On one occasion—and I have relived every second of it a hundred times—alone with my two labradors I had thirteen head of game, which of itself is not impressive, but it included eleven varieties, which could happen nowhere else but Scotland. They were:

<table>
<tr><td>1 cock grouse</td><td>1 jack snipe</td></tr>
<tr><td>1 cock pheasant</td><td>1 full snipe</td></tr>
<tr><td>1 partridge</td><td>1 mallard</td></tr>
<tr><td>1 hare</td><td>1 teal</td></tr>
<tr><td>1 rabbit</td><td>2 grey lag geese.</td></tr>
<tr><td>2 woodcock</td><td></td></tr>
</table>

Although this book is about flying, not shooting, the two have much in common: eye, hand, footwork, good co-ordination, quick reactions, ability to judge speed, height and distance, an awareness of danger, an eye for country and compassion for the quarry.

Like most shooting men who have the opportunity, I suffered severely from goose fever, and used my aeroplane to further this disease.

A flying man can learn a lot from wild geese. One such lesson is "no see, no fly." Geese do not fly in fog, at least not from choice. In fog they cannot navigate and become disorientated, and occasionally they get caught out, just like pilots. This particularly happens to them on migration. In mid-October they begin to arrive on the estuaries, having flown all the way from Spitzbergen, Bear Island and other Arctic breeding grounds. They have to take a chance on the weather at destination, which is where trouble sets in.

One year twenty-seven dead geese were found at the bottom of Glen Cova, all with broken necks. They had flown, in fog or cloud, slap into the side of a mountain at 2000 feet. Just like aeroplanes.

On another occasion in Lincolnshire during the war, one very foggy night in early November we had the Sandra lights on to assist aircraft returning from operations. Sandra lights were searchlights positioned round the perimeter and directed upwards at an angle to cone over the middle of the airfield. The fog did not clear before morning, and throughout the whole of that night hundreds of geese in huge skeins orbited the Sandra lights waiting for daylight.

They too were on migration, and obviously making for the Wash. They were quite low and well within shot most of the time, but despite the fact that roast goose in wartime rationed Britain would have been an improvement on spam and dried egg, nobody attempted to shoot; it seemed so unfair. If you are going on a wild goose chase, it is right and proper to do it the hard way, on ground of their choosing, out on the marsh in a freezing dawn up to your hocks in mud, or lying on your back (to cast no shadow) in the middle of a Perthshire field of winter wheat under the moon at two o'clock of a January morning, with the recoil of the twelve-bore, which you wouldn't notice standing up, slamming your shoulder hard into the frozen ground. That is as it should be. Not when they are an easy target, lost and confused; which brings me to geese and Tiger Moths.

The Tay estuary every winter attracts, or did, about 30,000 geese in roughly equal proportions of Pink Feet and Grey Lag. Normally they stay out on the saltings all night and flight inland at daybreak to feed on winter wheat, frozen potatoes left behind after the crop has been lifted, and on good grassland. They can do a lot of damage. When there is a moon they change their routine and stay out on the estuary during the day and flight in at night to feed under the moon. These conditions were the ones in which I preferred to shoot, and the best time was after the first quarter but before the full moon. It was also necessary to have about four to five-eighths cloud, otherwise it was impossible to see them. They are invisible against a clear sky at night.

There are millions of acres of arable land on either side of the Tay estuary, so it is helpful to know where exactly geese are feeding, if you are not to spend all night motoring around looking and listening; which is where the Tiger Moth comes in.

The Tiger cruises at around 90mph, but can be flown quite happily at just above stalling speed, which means you can float about in it like a balloon, making hardly any noise. Thus you have an ideal goose reconnaissance vehicle. If not frequently disturbed, geese will return to the same grazing area day after day, or night after night, so all you had to do having located your raiding party by air recco was to return to base, telephone the farmer or land-

126

owner on whose ground the geese were feeding and ask if you might enter thereon. Permission was usually forthcoming. The geese were considered a pest, as woodpigeons are in more southerly latitudes.

Overseas again, Australia this time, on loan, as it was called, to the Royal Australian Air Force. With the rank of squadron leader I was appointed Chief Flying Instructor at the Point Cook Cadet College in Victoria, lying about ten miles from Melbourne with Port Philip Bay on one side of its peninsula and Bass Straight on the other.

Point Cook was, and is, the RAAF's Cranwell.

It is popularly supposed that discipline in the Australian fighting forces is slack to the point of non-existence. This supposition is entirely erroneous. Discipline at Point Cook was strict and punishment for wrongdoers swift and severe. The cadets and the unit as a whole prided themselves on their behaviour and turn-out, and could stand comparison with Cranwell, Sandhurst or any other military academy.

What was different about Australians was their attitude to anyone in authority who, in their judgement, appeared to be unfitted for the task he was trying to do, or who was what they called 'la-di-dah', whatever that means. They took it for granted that all Englishmen (pommy bastards) were effete and soft, that they couldn't drink without falling flat on their faces and that they couldn't stay on a bucking horse for longer than it took to get on to its back.

One soon learned that it was a waste of time to issue a direct order. Such methods invited immediate hostility and suspicion. Instead, if you wanted something done, perhaps differently from the way it had been done in the past, you would say, "Do you think it would be a good idea if we tried doing so and so in such and such a way?" And the reply would be, "Ah well, we'll give it a go." So you said, "OK, give it a go then, and let me know what you feel about it."

The great thing was never to ask an Australian to do anything you couldn't do yourself, and preferably a damn sight better.

There was argument at times between the station commander, Group Captain 'Black Jack' McCauley, and myself. We didn't always see eye to eye in matters pertaining to the flying programme, and here I apologise in advance for shooting another line. The one about the night forced landing in Kurdistan is bad enough, but what follows is an even bigger line-shoot, though I consider it necessary in order to emphasise my point.

Point Cook was equipped with Avro Cadets for ab initio training, and Hawker Demons (the fighter variant of the Hart) and Avro Ansons for service type instruction.

The flight commander of one of the Demon flights made a regular practice of performing aerobatics nearly every morning over the airfield and was looked upon as no end of a hero, yet a clumsier, more unpolished display of brute force and ignorance would have been hard to find.

I said nothing, but bided my time. The moment was not yet.

One day an Avro Cadet was due out of workshops after a major overhaul. The chief engineer officer asked if I would like to do the air test on it. "Yes," I said, "I would like to very much. How about you, would you like to come as passenger and see for yourself if the work is to your liking?" He said he would welcome the opportunity.

I carried out the standard test flight procedure, checking the way the Avro was rigged, the response to all controls, stick forces recovering from a dive, stalling speeds engine on and engine off, spin recovery, rate of climb, power settings, pressures, temperatures, all the usual things, but I especially wanted to get the measure of the aircraft.

It was time to put on a show. I cast my mind back to the day when D'Arcy Greig said, "See that Fury over there—everything you know", and decided to pull out all the stops.

I looped it, slow rolled it, barrel rolled it, upward rolled it, half rolled it off the top of a loop, rolled it through a steep turn, flew it upside down, spun it, spun it again inverted, flew it between the hangars, then did an inverted circuit and approach rolling out just over the airfield boundary, landed off that and took off again.

The entire station was out. All the troops from workshops and hangars, all the cadets from lecture rooms, the headquarters staff, the WAAF, even the women from married quarters. I climbed back to 1500 feet over the middle of the airfield, turned off the fuel, waited for the engine to cut, stalled the aircraft to stop the prop and did a dead stick landing on the tarmac.

There was complete silence. Everybody just stood there. Then the engineer warrant officer walked over with the serviceability sheet and asked, "How was she, sir?" "Nice aeroplane," I said, and walked to my office.

From that day on there was no more trouble. Black Jack concluded every discussion by saying, "You are the chief instructor, the flying is your responsibility," and we became good friends. I met the Chief of the Air Staff a few days later at a cocktail party. His only comment was, "I hear you showed 'em how to fly at Point Cook."

The Demon pilot (in both senses of the term), if he did any more aerobatics took good care to do them well out of sight and sound of the airfield.

Moral—don't ask an Aussie to do what you cannot do yourself.

Opportunities for shooting in Australia were few, mainly because areas that held game were a very long way away and entailed an expedition which needed to be planned weeks ahead. Rabbits of course were everywhere. The country in those pre-myxamatosis days was overrun with the pests. The airfield was no exception, especially an acre or two of rough ground overgrown with thistles, nettles, thorn and scrub.

Walking back to my quarters after shooting four rabbits there one evening, I was greeted by one of the Australians.

"Good on yer, cobber, where did y'get 'em?"

"Over there," I pointed.

"Holy cow, you stupid bloody pom, you're lucky to be alive! It's crawling with tiger snakes," he said. "Never go in there or any place like that unless you are wearing breeches and knee-high boots."

I was wearing khaki shorts and shoes.

There was black duck shooting in the swamps and water holes along the Murrumbidgee river. You flew up to Narrandera, where one of the RAAF officers had made the arrangements, then piled all your gear and a week's supply of food—they didn't do things by halves: chops, steaks, onions, potatoes, eggs, bacon, bread, beans, coffee, butter, milk, tea and crates of beer—into a station wagon, and just drove across country—no roads—until you reached a likely area, where you made camp, building a very big fire which was never allowed to go out till you struck camp. The best steak or chop in the world is one grilled over a eucalyptus wood fire.

But there was one form of shooting which I have not seen anywhere else before or since. This was shooting quail over pointers from the back of a horse, and in the doing of it the reason for this method became clear. Quail country is the open plain, sparsely covered with grass and scrub, typical Merino sheep grazing. The quail are not plentiful, perhaps a covey to 500 acres, so the amount of ground to be covered if you hoped to kill three or four brace in a day is vast. To four guns, who hunted in pairs, there were four couples of pointers, which were carried until wanted, and again after they had done their share, in a large station wagon. The guns split into two teams, each working one pair of dogs, who hunted fast and ranged wide and more often than not came to a point a quarter of a mile or more away. If you were on foot it would seldom be possible to reach a point before the birds flushed. Bird dogs cannot hold a point indefinitely hence, apart from the distances involved, the need for horses. When you reached the point and the quail were flushed, you did not dismount, but shot from the saddle over the pony's head. Australian stock ponies are wonderful rock-steady animals, though they always buck for five minutes when you first mount. They never need to be tethered. You just drop the reins (which can be unbuckled) on to the ground and so long as the reins are hanging from the bit the ponies just stand there; so you took both barrels at the flushed birds and the only indication the ponies gave of having noticed was a slight twitch of the ears. The pointers retrieved and delivered to hand by standing on their hind legs with their fore-paws on the pony's flank. At lunch-time the first two pairs of dogs went back into the station wagon and the second two worked the afternoon shift.

The rice paddies around Mildura on the Victoria-South Australia border also provided wild fowling, with black duck, teal and pygmy geese. Expeditions to this area were chiefly remarkable for the incredible prowess of the eight year old son of one of the farmers. This child shot high-flying duck with a .22 rifle with deadly precision, making grown men with twelve-bore shotguns look very red in the face.

Before leaving Australia I had the good fortune to meet Professor Cotton of Sydney University, which meeting indirectly influenced my posting to the Royal Aircraft Establishment, Farnborough.

It is here necessary to compress time. I had intended this

130

narrative to be confined strictly to the ten years up to the outbreak of war, whereas Farnborough was a wartime stint. Aircraft were now being produced with performances which severely tested the capabilities of the individual, and Cotton, the boffin, had been working on the problem of how to overcome the limitations of the human body, particularly the effects of centrifugal force when manoeuvring at high speed. This loading is measured in terms of gravity, or G.

A loading of 3G is equal to a force three times that of gravity, or to put it another way, if you normally weigh twelve stone, at 3G you weigh thirty-six stone. In flight this force acts in a head-to-foot direction and values of around 5G for five seconds can cause the pilot to black out, because blood is drained from the head and eyeballs.

Tolerance of G varies between individuals and even in the same individual from day to day.

A reasonably fit pilot ought to be able to tolerate $4\frac{1}{2}$G without too much distress, but his ability to withstand it is decreased by fatigue, hunger, illness (even a cold) and especially by a hangover; equally, the individual can increase his tolerance to high G forces by practice, by keeping fit, and when flying, by straining and tightening the stomach muscles, and also by raising the legs or lowering the seat and at the same time crouching forward—in other words, by reducing his seated height.

Spitfires had an elevated rudder pedal about four inches above the normal rudder pedal, to enable pilots to raise their legs, and also the seat could be lowered.

Cotton devised a flying suit which could be progressively filled with compressed air. The suit was plugged into the air compressor which provided power for the wheel brakes, flaps, radiator flaps and guns. Through a complicated system of automatic valves the suit exerted pressure first around the ankles of the wearer and then, as G progressed, spread the pressure until finally the whole of the lower limbs, then the abdomen and finally the ribs just below the heart were squeezed as by a bear hug, thus preventing the blood from being forced away from the brain and heart. The pressure exerted was one pound per square inch per G.

Cotton, like all boffins, had tremendous faith in his own theories. There was a shark problem in all Australian waters, notably the Timor sea which separates tropical Australia from New Guinea.

Pilots ditching in the Timor or bailing out over it hadn't got a hope in hell of surviving. Cotton worked on this problem also and finally produced from his test tubes a solution which, if applied to flying clothing, would repel any shark, including the tiger shark and that most deadly of all, the grey nurse.

The initial demonstration of the repellent-treated flying suit was arranged to take place in one of the many shark-infested lagoons along the coast of the Northern Territory. The professor, surrounded by politicians, service chiefs and sceptical pilots, donned his flying suit and was about to jump into the water when one of the pilots shouted, "Hold it, Professor, 'gators!"

Cotton, with only momentary hesitation, not having given any thought to alligators until that moment, said, "This stuff will scare them too", and jumped in.

Several alligators immediately started to close in on him, and to the amazement of the by now horrified spectators, got within about ten yards then turned around and swam away. A most convincing demonstration.

CHAPTER 10

The time will come, when thou shalt lift thine eyes
To watch a long drawn battle in the skies,
While aged peasants, too amazed for words
Stare at the flying fleets of wond'rous birds.

Gray, Luna Habitabilis, *1797*

My departure from the RAAF Cadet College at Point Cook marked the end of a long association with flying training, except for a brief period during the war when I commanded a station whose function was to provide refresher training for Navy pilots on an odd assortment of aircraft, including the Swordfish, that famous (or infamous, depending on the point of view) 'Stringbag' that crippled the battleship *Bismarck*, and the Mercury-engined Miles Master fighter trainer, one of Miles' less successful designs.

I shed no tears at ceasing to be a sort of airborne schoolmaster. Much as I had wanted to be a flying instructor when I left Iraq, I had now had a bellyful. Two thousand eight hundred flying hours on Tutors, Cadets, Tiger Moths, Harts, Hinds, Demons, Magisters, Harvards, Ansons, Oxfords, even Battles, devoted almost exclusively to teaching people to fly, teaching instructors to instruct, or directing the activities of others at the task, had become a downright bore. Yet it had had its moments of high comedy, near-disaster and miraculous, if quite undeserved, escapes from what ought to have been certain death for the performers.

There were the two Tiger Moths at Filton, each with an instructor and pupil on board. One was on instrument training with the pupil under the hood and flying just below the cloud base. The other was descending and hit the one below as he broke cloud. The two in the upper aircraft bailed out safely, but the pupil under the hood in the bottom aircraft couldn't get out. The instructor did his damndest but finally decided that if he was going to go he had better go now. By this time he had insufficient height for his parachute to open, but he jumped anyway. He pulled the rip cord, his chute opened at ground level, and by a million to one chance lowered him into the bottom of a disused quarry.

There was the Anson in Scotland which, flying happily and

steadily at 2000 feet in cloud, ground gently to a standstill. The astonished crew, with their altimeter reading 2000 feet and all the other instruments at zero, peered fearfully out through the murk, wondering whether to bail out, and could just discern heather. They had belly-landed at full flying speed on the very, very slightly rising top of a grouse moor in Perthshire.

Two Ansons were involved in a remarkable accident at Wagga in Australia, in very similar circumstances to the Tiger Moths at Filton. Each was being flown by a student pilot with another navigating. One was just below cloud, a silly place to be, whilst the other was just in it but losing height. The upper aircraft hit the lower one and the propeller tips of each pair of engines cut into and locked solid on to the Townend rings of the other pair. The two cadets in the upper aircraft lost no time in bailing out, but the pilot of the lower one, finding he had a measure of control, decided to stay put and carry out standard forced landing procedure, and in pick-a-back configuration landed both Ansons on the belly of the lower one, thus saving the Australian Air Force £40,000.

At Point Cook one of my instructors, Tony Robinson, flying an ancient Wapiti—there were still a few about in the RAAF—with a cadet on board, was sliced into by another which sheared the starboard main-planes clean off. The Wapiti naturally went into a high rate of rotation spin. The cadet bailed out successfully but Tony pulled his rip cord too soon and the canopy, as it streamed, wrapped itself round the empennage. Tony was of course for all intents and purposes a dead man, and he knew it. In fact he was swinging like a pendulum from the tail of the Wapiti and just happened to be on the upswing as the aircraft hit the ground, thus only suffering the effect of falling from a height equivalent to the length of the shroud lines. He was badly smashed up but did fully recover, only to be killed on operations back in England.

The last incident I should like to record concerned two student pilots flying, one as pilot, the other as navigator, on a three-leg navigation exercise from Montrose. The first leg along the coast and the other two out to sea and back to base. They lost themselves and, seeing a ship down below, the pilot told the navigator that he would fly alongside the ship as low as possible and that he, the navigator, was to jump into the sea. The ship would of course stop, put out a boat and bring the intrepid airman aboard, whereupon he was to request the captain to point his ship towards

Montrose and the pilot would then set a similar course, return to base and report.

Believe it or not, it all went as planned. This idiot did jump into the sea from an aircraft flying at about 120 knots and suffered no ill, but the pilot, watching all this and flying in tighter and tighter orbit, did what had so often been done before and spun in off a steep turn. The captain yet again put a boat out and rescued this budding ace just a fraction before his aircraft sank. The ship was a Greek freighter on passage to Oslo for a load of timber and salt herring. No one on board had any English and even if they had, it is unlikely that they would have put about to land our precious pair in Scotland.

And so to Farnborough, or more precisely to the Physiological Laboratory, RAE Farnborough.

Generally Farnborough test pilots belonged to the Aircraft Establishment. The pilots in the phys. lab. were all flying doctors. Doctors first, pilots second. They subjected themselves to their own experiments in their own aircraft. The administrative staff addressed them all, including me, as 'doctor'. My repeated disclaimer was just as repeatedly ignored. We were equipped with a selection of Spitfires, mostly Mk IXs, but also a Mk XIII and a Mk VIII with clipped wings and a cropped supercharger, known for short as 'clipped, cropped and clapped'—i.e. clapped out. There was also a Hurricane and an old Fairey Battle, the rear cockpit of which was equipped with a battery of cine cameras remotely controlled from the front, so that a complete film record could be made of what happened to a passenger when not protected from high G forces, when deprived of oxygen, when not wearing protective clothing, or any number of other situations. No one but a flying doctor was ever asked to undergo this torture.

Farnborough had a station defence flight of Spitfire IXs with which we were supposed to fend for ourselves when attacked. This only happened twice while I was there, when we came under daylight low-level strafing attack from intruder Me110s.

The main function of the defence Spitfires was to fly fighter cover for any of our captured enemy aircraft, or any odd-looking aircraft such as Willie's Gloster Twin.

Despite the fact that all EA at Farnborough were repainted in RAF livery, there was always a risk every time they flew of their being attacked by our own fighters. Not by the British, but by the Poles, the Czechs and the Free French. Especially the trigger happy Poles—they would recognise the silhouette and attack, without noticing the RAF markings or even caring. The brief to the fighter cover pilot was simple:

"Don't let any silly bugger shoot us down."

You were expected to achieve this happy state without firing your own guns, so generally you interposed yourself between the attacker and the attacked and hoped that the 'silly bugger' would recognise another Spitfire when he saw one and draw the proper conclusions.

Anybody who was handy and not doing anything special at the moment got landed with this task, so say for example Roly Falk was going to fly the Ju88, he would ring the phys. lab., having perhaps tried everywhere else, and say, "Are you flying this morning, old boy?" Old boy would confess that no he wasn't, not till late afternoon.

"Good, then you wouldn't mind flying fighter cover for me?"

It was all very matey and casual.

You would like to fly a Spitfire? Well, get your gear and we will go over to dispersal, where I'll show you the taps and knobs and give you a cockpit check.

Here we are then. You can take MA477; she is an F Mk IX with the Merlin 61 engine. We'll go over the instrument panel first, then all the controls, switches, levers and knobs from left to right (see illustrations).

1. Ignition switches.
2. Undercarriage indicator.
3. Oxygen regulator.
4. Navigation lamps switch.
5. Flap control.
6. Instrument flying panel.
7. Lifting ring for sunscreen.
8. Reflector sight switch.
9. Reflector sight base.
10. Voltmeter.
11. Cockpit ventilator control.
12. Engine-speed indicator.
13. Supercharger warning lamp.
14. Boost gauge.
15. Intercooler protector pushbutton.
16. Coolant temperature gauge.
17. Oil temperature gauge.
18. Fuel pressure warning lamp.
19. Fuel contents gauge and pushbutton.
20. Oil pressure gauge.
21. Engine starter pushbutton.
22. Booster-coil pushbutton.
23. Cockpit floodlight switches.
24. Elevator tab position indicator.
25. Brake triple pressure gauge.

136

26. Crowbar.
27. Rudder trimming tab handwheel.
28. Pressure-head heater switch.
29. Two-position door catch lever.
30. Elevator trimming tab handwheel.
31. Throttle lever friction adjuster.
32. Floodlight.
33. Throttle lever.
34. Undercarriage indicator master switch.
35. Propellor speed control.
36. T.R.1133 pushbutton control.
37. Slow-running cut-out.
38. Signal discharger pre-selector control.
39. Signal discharger firing control.
40. Power failure lamp.
41. Radiator ground test pushbutton.
42. Supercharger ground test pushbutton.
43. Oil dilution pushbutton.
44. Map case.
45. Rudder pedal adjusting starwheel.
46. Propellor control friction adjuster.
47. Fuel cock control.
48. Engine priming pump.
49. Signalling switchbox.
50. Fuel tank pressure cock.
51. Remote contactor and contactor switch.
52. Undercarriage control lever.
53. IFF pushbuttons.
54. Harness release control.
55. IFF master switch.
56. Undercarriage emergency lowering control.
57. Rudder pedal adjusting starwheel.
58. Drop tank cock control.
59. Drop tank jettison lever.
60. Windscreen de-icing cock.
61. Seat adjustment lever.
62. Windscreen de-icing needle valve.
63. Windscreen de-icing pump.
64. Microphone/telephone socket.
65. Oxygen supply cock.

All right so far? Good. Now to start up.
1. Main tank fuel cock ON.
2. Magneto switches OFF.
3. Main tank booster pump ON for starting, take-off and landing; OFF during flight.
4. Check undercarriage selector lever DOWN.
5. Check indicator light shows green.
6. Tanks are full, but check contents anyway.
7. Test flying controls—ailerons, elevators and rudder.
8. Set propeller control lever fully FORWARD.

9. Set throttle lever ½in to 1in open and tighten friction.
10. Set supercharger lever to NORMAL AUTOMATIC.
11. Set carburettor air intake filter control to CLOSED.
12. Prime engine with 4–5 strokes on the Ki-gass pump or until pump becomes stiff to operate.
13. Switch on both magneto switches and press the starter button AND the booster coil button at the same time.
14. Release the starter button when she starts but keep the booster coil button pressed until she is running evenly.
15. Screw down the priming pump then open up gradually to 1,200rpm and warm up at that.
16. Check that the fuel pressure warning light does not come on.
17. Test all services while warming up.
18. Check temperatures and pressures.
19. Press radiator flaps test pushbutton and have ground crew check flaps open.
20. Test each magneto in turn.
21. Warm up to at least 15°C oil temperature and 60°C coolant temperature.
22. Open up to zero boost 0 lb/sq in and check operation of the two stage two speed supercharger.
23. Red light should come on when high gear is engaged.
24. At the same boost exercise and check the operation of the constant speed propeller by moving the lever over its full range then return lever to fully forward.
25. Check generator is charging.
26. Again check each magneto in turn. The drop on either mag should not exceed 150rpm.
27. See that two men are on the tail-plane, then open throttle to take-off setting and check boost and static rpm.
28. Throttle back until rpm falls just below take-off figure, to ensure that propeller is not constant speeding.
29. Before taxiing out check brake pressure (80lb/sq in) and pneumatic pressure (220lb/sq in).

For take-off:
1. Trim tabs. Elevator neutral. Rudder fully right; she swings left on take-off.
2. Propeller control: Lever fully forward.
3. Fuel: Main tanks cock ON. Booster pump ON.

138

4. Flaps UP.
5. Supercharger: Switch AUTO NORMAL (red light out).
6. Carburettor air intake filter control CLOSED.
   You will find that plus 7lb/sq in to plus 9lb/sq in of boost is OK for take-off but increase it to plus 12lb/sq in on the climb, otherwise you will get lead fouling of the plugs.
7. Select undercart UP and hold selector lever hard forward till red warning light comes on.
8. You will find the trimming tabs powerful and sensitive in flight, so use with care at high speed. Changes of trim occur as follows:
9. Undercarriage up. Nose up.
10. Undercarriage down. Nose down.
11. Flaps up. Nose up.
12. Flaps down. Nose strongly down.

She stalls engine off at 93mph wheels and flaps up, and 80 wheels and flaps down. You will get a stall warning of tail buffeting at 10mph above the stall. She stalls quite gently but one wing will drop.

Spin her if you want to, but not below 10,000 feet, and don't do more than two full turns before recovery. Let the speed on the recovery dive build up to 180mph before pulling out, otherwise she will flick into another spin.

Maximum permissible speed in a dive at any height between sea level and 20,000 feet is 450mph, and with flaps or undercart down 160mph. Maximum continuous cruise settings are 2650rpm plus 7 boost, 105°C coolant temperature and 90°C oil temperature.

If you feel like throwing her about, the minimum speeds for entry are, Loop 300mph; Half roll off the top 340mph; Slow roll 240mph; Upward roll 330mph.

Before landing reduce speed to 160mph and check: a. Sliding canopy—OPEN and LOCKED; b. Undercarriage—DOWN. Green light ON; c. Propeller control—Set to give 2650rpm (fully forward); d. Supercharger—Red light OUT; e. Fuel—Main tanks ON. Main tanks booster pump ON; f. Flaps—DOWN; g. Brakes —Check pressure 80lb/sq in.

If you are doing a gliding approach bring her in at 135–140mph, then reduce this crossing the airfield boundary to 110–115 flaps up,

and 100–105 flaps down, and go easy with the brakes after landing.
Have you got all that?

You have?

Good.

Off you go then and have fun.

See you in the bar at lunchtime.

I was posted to Farnborough to conduct experiments in G forces, with and without protection, in negative G, for which there wasn't any protection anyway, and to report on the relative merits of two types of anti G protective flying clothing: the Cotton air gradient suit and the Franks water-filled suit. The Cotton I have already discussed. The Franks, also taking its name from its designer, was a simpler device, being merely a double-skinned flying suit of water impervious material, which the pilot donned and climbed into his aircraft, whereupon a ground crewman filled it through a funnel from cans of water. You then screwed the stopper tight, like a hot water bottle, and away you went.

As the G increased so the water was pushed by centrifugal force down to the lower limbs and exerted sufficient pressure to counter-act the concentration of blood in the legs and abdomen.

I hated the Franks suit. It was cold and clammy and always made me want to piddle after half an hour's flying. Micturate, we 'medical' men called it—you couldn't write a rude word like piddle in an official report—but the Navy test pilots swore by the suit, so we agreed to differ. I suppose it was more their element. Obviously they felt thoroughly at home surrounded by water.

During this period at the phys. lab., my standard unprotected tolerance of $4\frac{1}{2}$G gradually crept up to $6\frac{1}{2}$ without blacking out and, wearing the Cotton suit, 8 to $8\frac{1}{2}$ was commonplace, thus amply demonstrating that a fighter pilot so protected would have an immense advantage over an adversary not similarly equipped.

Negative G is a very different matter. It acts in a foot to head direction, so you get a 'red-out' as the blood is forced into the upper body and finally the head and eyeballs fill, and very un-pleasant it is. But the experiments in this case had little or nothing to do with seeking a solution to the pilot's physical problem. You could not very well put his head in a bag and squeeze it.

Good as the Spitfire and Hurricane were, and superb as the Merlin engines of all marks were, they still relied on conventional float-type carburettors. The engines in the Me109 and later in the Fw190 had fuel injection, consequently they could bunt straight into a dive from level flight without loss of power. If you did that in a Spitfire or Hurricane the engine, starved of fuel, would cut out, preventing the pilot from following the EA down except by rolling into the dive, by which time it would be too late; so what we were experimenting with at Farnborough was fuel injection. These tests eventually led to the introduction of the Bendix Stromberg injection carburettor, fitted to later marks of Rolls Royce engines, notably the Merlin 66, 70 and 266.

The best way of obtaining maximum negative G, without wasting a lot of time losing height and clambering all the way up again, was to climb steeply on full power and then shove the stick hard forward. It was rather like reaching the peak of a very steep mountain and falling straight down the reverse slope.

It was unpleasant but not dangerous; at least it needn't have been. However, at Farnborough all aircraft maintenance was done by civilian ground engineers, which in itself is not a criticism, but if anything went wrong with your aircraft or engine through faulty maintenance it was no good complaining about it. You just had to lump it. If you tried to pursue it, that would be victimisation and they might all go on strike.

What happened to me in the first of such incidents was that, as I bunted the Spit into its negative G sequence, some heavy object shot up from the bottom of the cockpit, giving me a hammer-like blow on the cheek bone as it flashed past my head, hit the perspex canopy with a crash and then, as the G came off and Newton took over, fell back into the control box from which the stick grew; there was I, with the stick jammed fully to port and the aeroplane doing non-stop slow rolls to the left. One could prevent it going into a high speed spiral dive with trim tab, but the more I messed about with the stick the worse it became, and I decided that if only I could persuade the wretched aircraft to stay on its back long enough, whatever was jamming the controls might fall out again. It was either that or bailing out, if I could get out.

Then inspiration came, as it always does when you are in trouble; next time round, let go of the blasted stick entirely and see what happens. It worked. The obstruction fell out, hitting me on the chin this time, and I managed to field it with both hands. It was one of those big adjustable spanners which are not supposed to be used on aircraft. At that moment I could have used that spanner on its owner with the greatest relish.

My second brush with civilian maintenance could have had unfortunate results, because there was less height and therefore less time.

I never used flaps on the approach to land in a Spitfire until the very last minute. Because of the great big nose—like a Ninak—obscuring the view, I always came in on a continuous slipping turn so that, with the inner wing down and the nose slewed up and outwards, I could see where I was going, and I only selected flaps down as I slid over the boundary at 50 feet and lined up with the runway. On this occasion the moment flaps down was selected the Spit started a violent roll to starboard but, because one was in constant flying practice, one knew instinctively what had happened. Only one flap had functioned. You knew it was not aileron trouble, because you could see those from the cockpit, so your mind's eye took in the entire external configuration of the aircraft in the space of a micro-second, your hand flashed straight back to the switch and you selected flaps up; the Spit righted itself with ten feet to spare and I landed it at 95mph, cursing and too angry to be scared. Some clown had failed to carry out his proper maintenance checks.

I wasn't the only victim. One of the pilots was faced with a similar situation in a Hampden bomber. He put it into a steep turn and there the damn thing stayed, with jammed ailerons, but like most test pilots he got out of trouble somehow, and when the wings were opened up during the subsequent inspection, a half-gallon can of aircraft dope and two brushes were found inside the port wing.

So, from Avro 504s to Spitfires in one decade, and we were again at war with Germany.

The golden age of the biplane was over, an era had passed, but the lessons learned from it were now being applied. The big men, the men of vision, had been there all the time. John Salmond, exponent of air control; Robert Brooke Popham, eminent staff college commandant during the formative years; Arthur Saundby, pioneer of heavy bomber strategy and techniques; Longmore, who developed torpedo dropping from aircraft; Ralph Sorley, who gave us eight guns in our fighters instead of only two; John Slessor, scholar and strategist; Stuffy Dowding, whose Fighter Command was soon to be tested in the fire and not found wanting; Arthur Tedder, and of course Charles Portal, who became chief of the Air Staff and remained so throughout the war.

They had been there planning, building, fighting the politicians and moulding their tiny little 32,000-strong airforce into an organisation that formed the bare bones of what at its World War II peak became a fighting force of one and a half million men.

So if I have given the impression that the service was officered entirely by overgrown schoolboys, I must make amends by pointing out that what people did on the ground and off duty bore little resemblance to how the same young men behaved in the air.

With very few exceptions, pilots flew their aircraft with a professional toughness and expertise of which they were proud, and had a right to be.

The thoroughly irresponsible and utterly reckless pilot was a rare bird, and if not weeded out early in his career, he almost invariably sooner or later weeded himself out in a very final if inglorious fashion.

Military aviation was not a suitable area for the employment of regimented automatons trained to do things by numbers. Air warfare, and particularly air fighting, was very much a matter of the skill, experience, courage and tenacity of one man and his aircraft pitted against another, so those far-sighted men, the senior commanders, looked with a tolerant though not always approving eye on the escapades of the pilots in the squadrons.

They never forgot that they too had once been young.